Celebrating Women

Celebrating Women

EDITED BY

Sarah Gristwood

BATSFORD

CONTENTS

FOREWORD

FOREWORD

The happiest women, like the happiest nations, have no history.

From *The Mill on the Floss*, 1860 | George Eliot (1819–1880)

From *My Muse*

Why does my Muse only speak when she is unhappy?
She does not, I only listen when I am unhappy
When I am happy I live and despise writing
For my Muse this cannot but be dispiriting.

Stevie Smith (1902–1971)

There is nothing more silly than to be too wise to be happy.

Lady Mary Wortley Montagu (1689–1762) to her sister Lady Mar, November 1726

The idea for this book came several years ago, when I was editing *Secret Voices*, an anthology of women's diaries. The material there was quite extraordinary, from explorers to exploited, from housewives to history-makers, lovers to lyricists. But, overall, the one thing the diary entries tended not to be was... happy?

I hope I managed to avoid the book becoming gloomy. To find entries where women recorded their joy. But it was not easy. Yes, of course the diary is in some ways a particular form – women are most likely to use this private space to express their frustrations and depression. But even looking further afield, the issue doesn't go away.

As women, we often relate to each other through shared difficulties. In past centuries, men's writing on women tended to be about what was wrong with them; feminist writing about how wrong men had made women feel. Women have historically hesitated to express any sense of achievement or joy. Partly on the Chinese principle – crying out 'bad rice' if the harvest is good, lest the gods be jealous and destroy you. Partly because many of the triggers for pleasure or celebration – appetite (satisfied), ambition (achieved) – have been traditionally disapproved of in us.

Friend after friend, when I was compiling these quotes and asked for their suggestions, began by saying airily, 'Oh, there must be thousands...' Friend after friend, after leafing through the library inside their heads, came back to me with a different 'Oh...' – of disillusionment, and understanding. The more so since this book is about women celebrating all it means to be a woman. The only extracts coming from men are the tribute paid by her husband to the Victorian cookery writer Mrs Beeton, at the end of her book – and, in so far as we assume male authors, the Biblical story of Ruth and Naomi.

The opening chapter, 'Firsts', reflects how far women have come. From being allowed to speak publicly or to write, to being allowed to vote – or being the one for whom the vote is cast. What seems revolutionary to one generation may seem commonplace to the next – which is why this chapter sees the quotes arranged in roughly chronological order.

The great, the historic, achievements open up a world of possibility to us all – but myriad individual women have carried on the fight, every day, in their own small way. I make no apology for including a few other, more personal, firsts – and, particularly, one unexpected liberation, the power of movement, that a surprising number of women celebrated in their writing, and with glee.

The first half of the twentieth century – when women's mobility, and their other freedoms, were exploding in tandem – was the age of the aviatrix; and when an Amelia Earhart or a Beryl Markham took to the skies, they carried all women's aspirations with them. But down on the ground, many more were delighted to reject the traditional injunction that women should stay at home and be still. Indeed, as late as 1973, Erica Jong's groundbreaking novel hailed for its open sexuality was called *Fear of Flying*, for her heroine Isadora Wing's fear of autonomy, fear of flying free.

The chapter begins with Valentina Tereshkova, the first woman in space, and Christine de Pizan, the first woman recorded as making a living by her pen. And then comes a quote that is a recently re-discovered 'first' by any standards – and which pushes the timescale of this anthology back by a millennium or three...

Some of the topics are obvious – 'Family', for one. Mothers, daughters, sisters. Often, out there on the front line of family relationships, we take them for granted because we can. Often, in literature as well as in life, these relationships have instead been idealized into unreality. But women's own writing tells a complex story. Families can be what we make them; some of the voices from whom we hear evoke broader family connections. But let's admit that one familial relationship carries perhaps more potential for controversy than any other. And for power, and for pleasure, too.

The mothers and daughters here acknowledge bonds – and define boundaries. They celebrate support, and they lament separation, whether physical or emotional. They express both pleasure and pain. And if there is one thing to be learned from the collective voice of the writers below, it must be this – that the maternal relationship, beyond all other, carries within it the potential for (the necessity of!) inevitable, if often hard-won, change. For discovery and self-discovery... As Nancy Friday famously put it, 'My Mother/My Self'.

Another obvious topic is 'Friends'. Since the dawn of the 1980s, female friendship has been the topic of the day. It has taken the starring role not only in studies and anthologies, but in blockbuster fiction and TV series, from *The Women's Room* to *Sex and the City* to Elena Ferrante. But it was not always this way.

Before those advances of feminism, men – by far the majority of published writers – were more likely to be uninterested in, or even threatened by, female friendship. Moreover, logistics and class division meant that (in the writing classes at least) a woman's friendship circle tended to centre around her family; as witness *Little Women* or *Pride and Prejudice*. (Though, that said, let's not forget Mrs Gaskell's 'Amazonian' world of Victorian *Cranford*, where the widows and spinsters support each other, and there is scarcely a man to be seen.)

But the pages and screens of the last half century are jam-packed with exalted female friendships. From political allies to party buddies, from helping with French lessons to holding your hair back when you throw up, a friend can indeed be (as one of her friends emailed the journalist Ruth Picardie in her last illness) 'the diary I never kept'.

There is more than one kind of friendship – and there is also, as Joan Armatrading sang, more than one kind of love. Some friendships between women given only platonic expression nonetheless come in the section entitled 'Falling in Love'. The appropriateness of that is a question women such as Vera Brittain discuss for themselves... 'Passionate friendships' are often attributed particularly to the eighteenth and nineteenth centuries, but they were surely alive and well in the sixteenth, when St Teresa of Avila lamented the closeness of nuns in her convent – and in the girls' stories of the early twentieth. This section also includes the element of friendship within a sexual partnership – or in a partnership after the sex has died out.

'Falling in Love' was the chapter that almost didn't happen. In a book by women and about women, is there really any place for a woman's passionate paean of praise to a man? It's true, it is hard to see it as celebratory when Sylvia Plath or Katherine Mansfield declare they are utterly incomplete (a mere eyelash) without their male lover; nor did the love so passionately expressed necessarily last, untarnished, forever.

But we have to remember that to these women themselves, their love, whether for a man or a woman, was their glory, not the weak spot in their armour. Even more importantly, women's right to express ardour and passion, to declare themselves publicly as sexual beings, has been hard won, and is indeed to be celebrated. It's no coincidence that in most traditional anthologies of, say, love letters, an overwhelming proportion of the entries are written by a man.

So we have writings between Vita Sackville-West and Virginia Woolf and, written in the same years, from Vita to her husband Harold. We have a letter from Virginia to Violet Trefusis – passion passing into friendship over the years – and the resoundingly sexual diary entries of Vita's mother, describing her marriage, a few decades before.

Some chapters may be less obvious. A chapter on 'Feasts and Festivity', in a book celebrating women? But I could easily have compiled a whole book on women celebrating – and, crucially, celebrating themselves through – food. This book, moreover, is about pleasure, and transcribing these extracts brought me a lot of it!

The kitchen has traditionally been a woman's sphere. Sometimes, no doubt, it has been her mere place of work, or even her prison – Shirley Conran's original tag for her groundbreaking *Superwoman* was that 'life is too short to stuff a mushroom.' But the kitchen has also been a woman's pleasure-palace, her place of supremacy – and of connection with generations of women ahead and before.

There is of course a long tradition of female-authored cookery books, from Mrs Beeton to Nigella Lawson, Elizabeth David, Delia Smith, and so many more. But it was with a thrill of surprise that I found *The Barbara Pym Cookbook* – not authored by her as such, but putting recipes to extracts from her writings. In the extract on pages 93–94 from *The Sweet Dove Died*, the cakes epitomize the competition between two women, and the éclair-eater's ultimate defeat by the party who managed to snatch the *marron glacé*.

Pym is very far from the only one to utilize food as an allegory; as an expression of a female sensuality. Food features in women's writing as temptation and satisfaction, achievement and inheritance, and as a marker of important events. Elizabeth Gilbert's bestselling voyage of self-discovery was significantly titled *Eat, Pray, Love*; while in *Three Weeks* (a byword for daring in its day) the exoticism of the mysterious lady is epitomized by the exquisite dinner she orders. Nella Last's diary entry about her 'bony mutton' casserole celebrates her skill as well as the savour; while Kamala Harris's description of the food her mother cooked reflects both her mixed heritage, and the thinker she has become today.

Perhaps 'Fashion' – appearance – is a given, in a book about women. There's a reason we all love a Cinderella story and it isn't necessarily the fairytale ending. For me, at least, it's the transformation scene that comes before. I'd cheerfully swap Prince Charming for the glass slippers (well, if you threw in the ability to wear them without blisters, anyway).

Clothes can represent change, they can represent courage. Often, and most interestingly, they can represent a woman's finding the courage to change herself, without the need for any Fairy Godmother. And not clothes alone, as Coco Chanel points out... Virginia Woolf may not be wholly serious in describing her haircut as the most important event of her life since marriage, but there is no doubt the short crops of the 1920s reflected a major shift in social norms. The 'sex 'n' shopping' novel may be a phenomenon of the late twentieth-century, but women have long been (as Flora Poste puts it in *Cold Comfort Farm*), 'artists in living flesh'. Like it or lump it, this is a task of creation with which we all deal every day.

Virginia Woolf most famously linked finance and furnishings (in the 'Foundations' chapter) when she declared that in order to write, which for Woolf meant to live, a woman needed £500 a year and a room of her own. But Harriet Beecher Stowe was seeking her own room, years before... The space carved out and created within a home can be a woman's sanctuary. I'm not sure which of the rooms featured in the 'furnishings' section most appeals to you – Jenny Diski's blessedly blank white cabin? Elinor Glyn's 'barbaric' draperies and famous tiger skin? – but it's Maria's sheepskin rugs and bare boards from *The Little White Horse* that I have in my house to this day.

The ability to create your space depends, of course, on an income. Money, and how we make it, is also a part of this chapter – as too, perhaps unexpectedly, are flowers, and fur.

We've already seen how women's sensuality, their sense of pleasure or identity has often been expressed indirectly, almost surreptitiously. In *Divine Secrets of the Ya-Ya Sisterhood,* Sidda, from the youngest generation of Walker women, can express her creativity as a theatre director; her mother Vivi uses food to express her love; and it's a garden that shows the downtrodden and downtreading grandmother in a new light. Women gardeners and garden writers have almost as much of a tradition as the writers of cookery books; flowers were the friends of May Sarton's elected solitude; the symbol of unquenchable hope in Margaret Atwood's *The Handmaid's Tale.* For ladies of the writing classes, one of the occupations (and exhibitions) was always 'doing the flowers'.

But of course we have to remember, too, that flowers, flowering, have long been a metaphor for the unfurling not only of petals, but of a personality. As for fur... well, perish the thought that our animal supporters could have gone into the sections entitled 'Friends', 'Family', or indeed 'Falling in Love'! But for many of us they – like the houses we live in, or the financial means by which we support them – are indeed a bedrock, a foundation, of our lives.

My favourite word has always been 'eclectic', which is lucky, because it's hard to think of one that could better describe the collection of quotes in this anthology. Poems, novels, memoirs and letters – cookbooks, and celebrity quotations. And had this been an album rather than an anthology, I could have included so many other voices, from the Spice Girls telling any potential lover he had to square it with their friends – or Annie Lennox pointing out that sisters were perfectly capable of doing it for themselves, Taylor Swift telling us we can do it on our own – or Lady Gaga that we should accept ourselves as we are, we were born that way. And Diana Ross would have been coming out, and Beyoncé would have been flawless ...

This is about women not only praising other women, but enjoying, appreciating being women – whether that's in the boardroom or the boudoir; in Parliament or at a party. The thing these extracts have in common is that they all show women as celebrated or celebrating; directly or indirectly. And my chief criterion was the hope that a quote I enjoyed transcribing was one you would enjoy reading.

From *Phenomenal Woman*

Pretty women wonder where my secret lies.
I'm not cute or built to suit a fashion model's size.

But when I start to tell them,
They think I'm telling lies,
I say,
It's in the reach of my arms,
The span of my hips,
The stride of my step,
The curl of my lips.
I'm a woman
Phenomenally.
Phenomenal woman,
That's me.

I walk into a room
Just as cool as you please,
And to a man,
The fellows stand or
Fall down on their knees.
Then they swarm around me,
A hive of honey bees.
I say,
It's the fire in my eyes,
And the flash of my teeth,
The swing in my waist,
And the joy in my feet.
I'm a woman
Phenomenally.
Phenomenal woman,
That's me.

Maya Angelou (1928–2014)

Mama exhorted her children at every opportunity to 'jump at de sun.' We might not land on the sun, but at least we would get off the ground.

From *Dust Tracks on a Road: An Autobiography*, 1942 | Zora Neale Hurston (1891–1960)

Let no weak fears, no timid doubts, deter you from the exertion of your duty, according to the fullest sense of it that Nature has implanted in your mind. Though gentleness and modesty are the peculiar attributes of your sex, yet fortitude and firmness, when occasion demands them, are virtues as noble and as becoming in women as in men...

Fanny Burney (1752–1840)

At last I saw that I too had been in the presence of great power, my mother talking-story. After I grew up, I heard the chant of Fa Mu Lan, the girl who took her father's place in battle. Instantly, I remembered that as a child I had followed my mother about the house, the two of us singing about how Fa Mu Lan fought gloriously and returned alive from war to settle in the village. I had forgotten this chant was once mine, given me by my mother, who may not have known its power to remind. She said I would grow up a wife and a slave, but she taught me the song of the warrior woman Fa Mu Lan. I would have to grow up a warrior woman.

From *The Woman Warrior*, 1975 | Maxine Hong Kingston (b.1940)

I am not afraid of storms, for I am learning how to sail my ship.

Louisa May Alcott (1832–1888)

Woman's Sphere

They talk about a woman's sphere as though it had a limit;
There's not a place in earth or heaven,
There's not a task to mankind given,
There's not a blessing or a woe,
There's not a whispered 'yes' or 'no',
There's not a life, or death, or birth,
That has a feather's weight of worth
Without a woman in it.

Kate Field (1838–1896)

All human life on the planet is born of woman.

Adrienne Rich (1929–2012)

'I was born to be a spinster and by God I'm going to spin.'

Winifred Holtby (1898–1935)

I am a forward-looking girl and don't stay where I am.

From *Novel on Yellow Paper*, 1936 | Stevie Smith (1902–1971)

Chapter 1
FIRSTS

FIRSTS

It is not easy to be a pioneer – but oh, it is fascinating! I would not trade one moment, even the worst moment, for all the riches in the world.

Elizabeth Blackwell, *first woman doctor in the USA* (1821–1910)

If women can be railroad workers in Russia, why can't they fly in space?

Valentina Tereshkova, *first woman in space* (b.1937)

Oh! What honour for the female sex! It is perfectly obvious that God has special regard for it ... the whole Kingdom now recovered and made safe by a woman, something 5000 men could not have done... Before the event they would scarcely have believed it possible.

Christine de Pizan (1364–1431) on Joan of Arc

Do not content yourself with small things. God wants great ones. If you become what you should be you will set all Italy and beyond aflame.

St Catherine of Siena (1347–1380)

From *The Exaltation of Inana*

Queen of vast heart,
wild last, proudest
among the Anuna.
Outstanding in all
lands, great daughter
of Nanna, eminent
among the Igigi.
Lady of glory, who
reaps the powers of
heaven and earth,
rival to mighty An.
It is she who rules
the gods, she who
seals their verdicts,
as the Anuna crawl
beneath her mighty
words. Even An does
not understand her
ways; he dares not go
against her orders...
Without Inana, An
Can reach no decisions,
Enlil can fix no fates.
Who can challenge a
queen who raises her
head higher than the
mountaintops? ... She
splits the blazing,
furious storm, the

whirlwind billows
around her as if
it were a dress.

Enheduanna, *priestess, the first named author in history* (c.2300BC)

A little girl of XVI (isn't this something beyond nature?) who does not even notice the weight of the arms she bears – indeed her whole upbringing seems to have prepared her for this, so strong and resolute is she! And her enemies go fleeing before her, not one of them can stand up to her. She does all this in full view of everyone, and drives her enemies out of France, recapturing castles and towns. Never did anyone see greater strength, even in hundreds or thousands of men! And she is the supreme captain of our brave and able men. Neither Hector nor Achilles had such strength! This is God's doing: it is he who leads her.

Christine de Pizan (1364–1431) on Joan of Arc

I am a woman, but I can assure you I am as brave as any man.

Nzinga, *ruler of Ndongo and Matamba, Angola* (c.1583–1663)

To be a king and wear a crown is a thing more glorious to them that see it than it is pleasant to them that bear it. For myself, I was never so much enticed with the glorious name of a king or the royal authority of a queen as delighted that God hath made me His instrument to maintain His truth and glory and to defend this kingdom (as I said) from peril, dishonour, tyranny and oppression. There will never queen sit in my seat with more zeal to my country, care to my subjects, and that will sooner with willingness venture her life for your good and safety, than myself. For it is not my desire to live nor reign longer than my life and reign shall be for your good. And though you have had and may have many princes more mighty and wise sitting in this seat, yet you never had nor shall have any that will be more careful and loving...

From Golden Speech (*final address to Parliament*), 30 November 1601 | Elizabeth I (1533–1603)

From the epilogue to *Sir Patient Fancy*

What has poor Woman done that she must be,
Debar'd from Sense and Sacred Poetrie?
Why in this Age has Heaven allow'd you more,
And Women less of Wit than heretofore?
We once were fam'd in Story, and cou'd write
Equall to men: cou'd Govern, nay cou'd Fight.
We still have passive Valour, and can show
Wou'd Custom give us leave the Active too,
Since we no provocations want from you...

Aphra Behn, *England's first professional woman writer* (1640–1689)

All women together ought to let flowers fall upon the tomb of Aphra Behn, which is, most scandalously but rather appropriately, in Westminster Abbey, for it was she who earned them the right to speak their minds. It is she - shady and amorous as she was - who makes it not quite fantastic for me to say to you tonight: Earn five hundred a year by your wits.

From *A Room of One's Own*, 1929 | Virginia Woolf (1882–1941)

Woman, wake up! The alarm bell of reason is making itself heard throughout the universe; recognize your rights. The powerful empire of nature is no longer beset by prejudices, fanaticism, superstition and lies. The torch of truth has dispelled all clouds of stupidity and usurpation. The enslaved man multiplied his forces but has had to resort to yours to break his chains. Once free he becomes unjust to his female companion. O women! Women, when will you stop being blind?

From *Declaration of the Rights of Woman and Citizen*, 1790 | Olympe de Gouges (1748–1793)

A wild wish has just flown from my heart to my head, and I will not stifle it though it may excite a horse-laugh. I do earnestly wish to see the distinction of sex confounded in society, unless where love animates the behaviour. For this distinction is, I am firmly persuaded, the foundation of the weakness of character ascribed to woman; is the cause why the understanding is neglected, while accomplishments are acquired with sedulous care: and the same cause accounts for their preferring the graceful before the heroic virtues ... should a more laudable ambition ever gain ground they may be brought nearer to nature and reason, and become more virtuous and useful as they grow more respectable...

From *A Vindication of the Rights of Woman*, 1792 | Mary Wollstonecraft (1759–1797)

'I hate to hear you talk about all women as if they were fine ladies instead of rational creatures. None of us want to be in calm waters all our lives.'

From *Persuasion*, 1817 | Jane Austen (1775–1817)

Wuthering Heights bears no definite feminine stamp – though perhaps only a woman could have liberated her spirit so completely. Charlotte Brontë's *Jane Eyre*, on the other hand, gains force by being woman from beginning to end. Made in this voice, the plain, proud, unhesitating assertion of woman's feeling for man – Jane's for Rochester – shocked the England of 1847. It had been the accepted idea that, while woman might, by very judicious degrees, respond to declared love, she did not initiate love on her own account – to do so was more than doubtful, it was 'unwomanly.' ... Jane wants much more than love; she wants human fullness of life – the book voiced, for the first time, woman's demand for this. Read the scene where, alone on the roof of the country house, Jane looks out over the country and cries for movement, achievement, adventure – feeling the masculine part of her spirit stir. Might this be called the first feminist novel?

From *English Novelists*, 1945 | Elizabeth Bowen (1899–1973)

She was an Amazon. Her whole life was spent riding at breakneck speed towards the wilder shores of love. For her, each new affair was an encampment set up along the way; sometimes a palace, sometimes a tent; but always the supreme refuge. She was not a nymphomaniac, however, for at each camp she seems to have believed the journey over. As it happened, it took her thirty-five years to reach her true destination, a fact she sometimes deplored as much as her detractors. After each heart-break there was a new dash, a new hope, and then, a new camp pitched hastily along the way. Too hastily, perhaps. But then, as some Mediterranean philosopher has said, life is three-quarters love, and Jane Digby loved life.

**From *The Wilder Shores of Love*, 1954 | Lesley Blanch (1904–2007)
on Jane Digby el Mezrab**

It is in vain that we would circumscribe the power of one half of our race, and that half by far the most important and influential. If they exert it not for good, they will for evil; if they advance not knowledge, they will perpetuate ignorance. Let women stand where they may in the scale of improvement, their position decides that of the race. Are they cultivated? – so is society polished and enlightened. Are they ignorant? – so is it gross and insipid. Are they wise? – so is the human condition prosperous. Are they foolish? – so is it unstable and unpromising. Are they free? – so is the human character elevated. Are they enslaved? – so is the whole race degraded. Oh! that we could learn the advantage of just practice and consistent principles...

From *Course of Popular Lectures*, 1828/9 | Frances Wright, *Scottish/American feminist* (1795–1852)

As to the use of the pen, there was quite as much opposition to Woman's possessing herself of that help to free agency as there is now to her seizing on the rostrum or the desk; and she is likely to draw, from a permission to plead her cause that way, opposite inferences to what might be wished by those who now grant it.

As to the possibility of her filling with grace and dignity any such position, we should think those who had seen the great actresses and heard the Quaker preachers of modern times would not doubt that Woman can express publicly the fullness of thought and creation, without losing any of the peculiar beauty of her sex.

From *Woman in the Nineteenth Century*, 1845 | Margaret Fuller, *first editor of a major US newspaper* (1810–1850)

Woman's stock is rising in the market. I shall not live to see women vote, but I'll come and rap on the ballot box.

Lydia Maria Child (1802–1880) to her fellow abolitionist and suffragist Sarah Shaw, 3 August 1856

If women want any rights more than they's got, why don't they just take them, and not be talking about it?

Sojourner Truth, *abolitionist* (c.1797–1883)

I am the seed of the free and I know it. I intend to bear great fruit.

Sojourner Truth (c.1797–1883)

Every great dream begins with a dreamer. Always remember, you have within you the strength, the patience, and the passion to reach for the stars to change the world.

Harriet Tubman, *abolitionist and activist* (1822–1913

I am very sorry you all thought me so rash and naughty in trying the ether. Henry's faith gave me courage, and I had heard such a thing had succeeded abroad, where the surgeons extend this great blessing much more boldly and universally than our timid doctors. Two other ladies, I know have since followed my example successfully, and I feel proud to be the pioneer to less suffering for poor, weak, womankind. This is certainly the greatest blessing of this age, and I am glad to have lived at the time of its coming and in the country which gives it to the world.

Fanny Longfellow, *wife of the Hiawatha poet Henry Wadsworth Longfellow and the first woman in America to make use of ether while giving birth* (1817–1861))

The young intellectuals are all chanting 'Revolution, Revolution,' but I say the revolution will have to start in our homes, by achieving equal rights for women.

Qiu Jin, ***Chinese poet and revolutionary*** **(1895–1907)**

Women's Rights

We want our emancipation!
For our liberty we'll drink a cup,
Men and women are born equal,
Why should we let men hold sway?

We will rise and save ourselves,
Ridding the nation of all her shame,
In the steps of Joan of Arc,
With our own hands we will regain our land.

Qiu Jin (AKA Jin Xiong, 'able to compete with men'), ***Chinese poet and revolutionary*** **(1895–1907)**

The young women of today, free to study, to speak, to write, to choose their occupation, should remember that every inch of this freedom was bought for them at great price. It is for them to show their gratitude by helping onward the reforms of their own time, by spreading the light of freedom and truth still wider.

Abigail Scott Duniway, ***suffragette*** **(1834–1915)**

Remember the dignity of your womanhood. Do not appeal, do not beg, do not grovel. Take courage, join hands, stand beside us, fight with us.

From speech at the Royal Albert Hall, 1909 | Christabel Pankhurst, *suffragette* (1880–1958)

I am striving to take into public life what any man gets from his mother.

Nancy Astor, *first serving female Member of Parliament* (1879–1964)

Motoring is a pastime for women: young, middle-aged, and - if there are any - old. There may be pleasure in being whirled around the country by your friends and relatives, or in a car driven by your chauffeur; but the real, the intense pleasure, the actual realisation of the pastime comes only when you drive your own car.

I have hunted - and was one of those who declare that the most glorious of all out-door life is in the saddle, on a fast, clean-jumping hunter; but when, by accident, I took up motoring I found the exhilaration, the delights of the gallop doubled. It fascinates me, and it will fascinate any woman who tries it.

From *The Woman and the Car*, 1909 | Dorothy Levitt, *first British woman racing driver* (1882–1922)

Now and then women should do for themselves what men have already done - occasionally what men have not done - thereby establishing themselves as persons, and perhaps encouraging other women towards greater independence of thought and action.

Amelia Earhart, *aviation pioneer and the first woman to fly solo non-stop across the Atlantic* (1897–1937)

We talk of nothing but cars...

...This is a great opening up in our lives. One may go to Bodiam, to Arundel, explore the Chichester downs, expand that curious thing, the map of the world in ones mind. It will I think demolish loneliness, & may of course imperil complete privacy... the motor is turning out the joy of our lives, an additional life, free & mobile & airy to live alongside our usual stationary industry... Soon we shall look back at our pre-motor days as we do now at our days in the caves.

Diary entries, 11 July and 10 August 1927 | Virginia Woolf (1882–1941)

But there were other doors to liberation. Flying was a very tangible freedom. In those days [the 1920s] it was beauty, adventure, discovery – the epitome of breaking into new worlds. From being earth-bound and provincial, I was given limitless horizons. From the cloistered atmosphere of books, writing and introspection, I was freed to action. The practical work of learning to fly, of being a radio operator and navigator, of carrying my own parachute and my own 'weight' as a crew member on the flights, gave me a feeling of tremendous self-confidence. For the first time, I had a sense of value in the 'real world' of life and action. Like the bird pushed out of the nest, I was astonished that – flapping hard – I could fly. All this was liberating.

From *Hour of Gold, Hour of Lead*, 1973 | Anne Morrow Lindbergh, *aviator* (1906–2001)

Please know that I am quite aware of the hazards. I want to do it because I want to do it. Women must try to do things as men have tried. When they fail, their failure must be but a challenge to others.

Amelia Earhart (1897–1937) to her husband, from her last letter before her plane disappeared over the Pacific, as she attempted to become the first female pilot to circumnavigate the globe, 1937

... It was even more disconcerting to examine your charts before a proposed flight only to find that in many cases the bulk of the terrain was bluntly marked: UNSURVEYED. It was as if the mapmakers had said, 'We are aware that between this spot and that one, there are several hundreds of thousands of acres, but until you make a forced landing there, we won't know whether it is mud, desert, or jungle – and the chances are we won't know then!'

From *West with the Night*, 1942 | Beryl Markham, *aviator* (1902–1986)

They were beyond proud of showing the Soviet Union that women could fly as well as any man.

Marina Raskova, *first woman navigator in the Soviet Air Force and commander of the all-female Night Witches regiment* (1912–1943)

Henrietta got the Delage out from the garage in the Mews and, after a wholly technical conversation with her friend Albert, who looked after the Delage's health, she started off.

'Running a treat, Miss,' said Albert.

Henrietta smiled. She shot away down the Mews, savouring the unfailing pleasure she always felt when setting off in the car alone. She much preferred to be alone when driving. In that way she could realise to the full the intimate personal enjoyment that driving a car brought to her.

She enjoyed her own skill in traffic, she enjoyed nosing out new short-cuts out of London. She had routes of her own and when driving in London itself had as intimate a knowledge of its streets as any taxi-driver.

From *The Hollow*, 1946 | Agatha Christie (1890–1976)

There in Paris, in July, 1936, I saw a brilliant platform of public women of all nations. To me as an old suffragette it was thrilling... in 1904 we [had been] told that although women might get the vote... not in our lifetime could we expect to see women in Parliaments and Governments, women in public office, women in all the professions. Such progress would not be possible for our generation – if ever.

And there in front of me on that Paris platform in July, 1936, were contingents of women parliamentarians from all countries... distinguished women doctors, lawyers, teachers, writers, artists... It had the effect on me of a revelation...

The magnificent regiment of women! Yes, I suddenly seemed to blink my eyes into and on to a new world at that Paris Congress in July 1936.

From *In Love with Life – A Pioneer Career Woman's Story*, 1944 | Beatrice Gordon Holmes, *stockbroker* (1884–1951)

I paved the way for all of them.

Alice Coachman, *first Black woman to win (in 1948) an Olympic Gold medal* (1923–2014)

Where, after all, do universal human rights begin? In small places, close to home ... Such are the places where every man, woman and child seeks equal justice, equal opportunity, equal dignity without discrimination. Unless these rights have meaning there, they have little meaning anywhere.

From speech to the United Nations, 1958 | Eleanor Roosevelt (1884–1962)

[My mother] had started a fresh chapter with astonishing courage after my father's death. It had grieved her very deeply indeed. But she had not bogged down in her past. She had taken advantage of the freedom that had been given back to her to rebuild a kind of life for herself that matched her own tastes. My father did not leave her a penny, and she was fifty-four. She passed examinations, attended courses, and she won a certificate that enabled her to work as an assistant librarian in the Red Cross. She learnt to ride a bicycle again to go to her office. She thought of doing dress-making at home after the war. When that time came I was in a position to help her. But idleness did not suit her. She was eager to live her own way at last and she discovered a whole mass of activities for herself.

From *A Very Easy Death*, 1964 | Simone de Beauvoir (1908–1986)

If they don't give you a seat at the table, bring a folding chair.

Shirley Chisholm, *first Black woman elected to the US Congress* (1924–2005)

The struggle which is not joyous is the wrong struggle. The joy of the struggle is not hedonism and hilarity, but the sense of purpose, achievement and dignity

From *The Female Eunuch*, 1969 | Germaine Greer (b.1939)

The second thing I noticed on our way to Locust Valley was the number of women driving cars. I am a driver from way back, I love good roads and good automobiles, and I noticed at once how many new cars were on the roads. But it was the variety of feminine types at the wheel that stuck me: pretty young girls, still almost children; smartly dressed women; many Negroes, young and old; women in furs and extraordinary big hats, like shrubs in bloom – and finally grey-haired women, for whom in the USSR the only possible vehicle would have been a wheelchair, driving cars expertly and with a certain dash, smoking a cigarette and chatting with a companion.

'A woman's health is the nation's health.' This was said by some sociologist back in the nineteenth century. These women behind the wheel, apparently the owners of the cars, looked charming, with their hair either cut short or long and flowing, their bright, slightly vulgar ornaments. No uniformity in style here, every woman looking the way she pleased. Many had two or three children with them, and dresses on hangers in the back of the car to avoid damaging them in suitcases. The good health, the freedom and independence of this young nation presented themselves graphically before my eyes on that hour's ride.

From *Abroad in America*, 1970 | Svetlana Alliluyeva (1926–2011), *daughter of Joseph Stalin, on her defection to the USA*

We have to be the change we want.

Jocelyn Bell Burnell, *astrophysicist, co-discoverer of the first radio pulsars* (b.1943)

This woman's place is in the House – the House of Representatives.

Bella Abzug, during her successful 1970 election campaign (1920–1998)

She is so clearly the best man among them.

Diary entry, 11 February 1975 | Barbara Castle (1910–2002)

You may have to fight a battle more than once to win it.

Margaret Thatcher, *Britain's first female Prime Minister* (1925–2013)

Think for a minute. Who were you before this wave of feminism began?...

New words and phrases are one organic measure of change. They capture transformations of perception, and sometimes of reality itself.

We have terms like sexual harassment and battered women. A few years ago, they were just called life.

Now, we are becoming the men we wanted to marry. Once women were trained to marry a doctor, not to be one.

Women's in front of words like center or newspaper, network or rock band, indicates a positive choice. Ten years ago, it was a put-down.

Now, we've made the revolutionary discovery that children have two parents. A decade ago, even the kindly Dr. Spock held mothers solely responsible for children.

In 1972, a NASA official's view of women's function in space was 'sexual diversion' [on] 'long-duration flights such as Mars.' Now, women are simply 'astronauts.'

From *Outrageous Acts and Everyday Rebellions*, 1982 | Gloria Steinem (b.1934)

Flying is suddenly miraculous! We dip and turn over the flats of Queens, where the inflated backyard swimming pools of the working-class row houses gleam like round blue eyes. I wish Leonardo da Vinci could be here beside me! If only he could ride in a 747! If only Jeannie could be here beside me, going off across the Rockies, going toward the big western sky, starting over, starting life over again.

Was it really Jeannie's death that suddenly released me from the fear of flying I'd had for years – or was it something else? Was it some new understanding of how uncontrollable life is, how little our anxieties influence our futures? Or was it suddenly growing up, growing unafraid of leaving home, leaving Mother, leaving the earth, leaving the street I grew up on, leaving Bennett, the man who made me 'Wing' and then tried to keep me from flying?

It was true, oddly enough, that even during all my worst panics about flying I dreaded takeoff and almost always enjoyed the landing. This was absurd because landing was, in fact, the most dangerous time. But perhaps what I really dreaded was leaving home – and suddenly leaving home was no longer terrifying. Home was wherever I was. And right now I was flying.

From *How to Save Your Own Life*, 1977 | Erica Jong (b.1942)

Evelyn and I climbed by ourselves for the next few days, choosing our own routes and belaying each other, and as each day drew to an end the realization came into clearer focus. I had learned the basics of climbing and had come to know I was strong enough and agile enough to eventually master the skills. I was surprised and delighted. I'd finally found something I wanted to focus my energy on. Something physical, where I could set goals and achieve things without having to compete with anyone else. Because more than anything, climbing was collaborative.

Learning to climb on the same rope with Evelyn locked out friendship in a much closer bond. She saw the same beauty in the sport, the same potential for personal revelation. With the same commitment, and the same base of physical strength, we worked hard together coaching, helping, and depending on one another for support. Evelyn and I didn't bother with limitations. Looking to each other for inspiration, we went ahead and learned what we needed to know.

From *Beyond the Limits*, 1993 | Stacy Allison, *first American woman to reach the summit of Mount Everest* (b.1958)

When anyone tells me I can't do anything... I'm just not listening any more.

Florence Griffith Joyner, *the fastest woman ever recorded* (1959–1998)

Feminism is the most revolutionary idea there has ever been. Equality for women demands a change in the human psyche more profound than anything Marx dreamed of. It means valuing parenthood as much as we value banking.

From the *Guardian*, 19 January 1987 | Polly Toynbee (b.1946)

won't you celebrate with me

'won't you celebrate with me
what I have shaped into
a kind of life? i had no model.
born in babylon
both nonwhite and woman

what did i see to be except myself?
i made it up
here on this bridge between
starshine and clay.
my one hand holding tight
my other hand; come celebrate
with me that everyday
something has tried to kill me
and has failed.

From *The Book of Light*, 1993 | Lucille Clifton (1936–2010)

Somewhere out in this audience may even be someone who will one day follow in my footsteps, and preside over the White House as the President's spouse. I wish him well!

From commencement speech, Wellesley College, 1990 | Barbara Bush (1925–2018)

The thing women have got to learn is that nobody gives you power. You just take it.

From *My Lives*, 1994 | Roseanne Barr (b.1952)

Being the first woman speaker and breaking the marble ceiling is pretty important. Now it's time to move on.

Nancy Pelosi, *US politician and former Speaker of the House of Representatives* (b.1940)

I ran as a daughter who benefited from opportunities my mother never dreamed of. I ran as a mother who worries about my daughter's future and a mother who wants to lead all children to brighter tomorrows. To build that future I see, we must make sure that women and men alike understand the struggles of their grandmothers and mothers, and that women enjoy equal opportunities, equal pay, and equal respect. Let us resolve and work toward achieving some very simple propositions: There are no acceptable limits and there are no acceptable prejudices in the twenty-first century.

You can be proud that, from now on, it will be unremarkable for a woman to win primary state victories, unremarkable to have a woman in a close race to be our nominee, unremarkable to think that a woman can be the President of the United States. And that is truly remarkable.

From concession speech after losing to Barack Obama in the Democratic primaries, 2008 | Hillary Rodham Clinton (b.1947)

To all those women, whom history and the severity of ruling systems have made unseen, to all women who made sacrifices for the sake of a healthy society with just relationships between women and men, to all those women who are still stumbling on the path of freedom in countries with no social justice or equal opportunities, to all of them I say: thank you ... this day wouldn't have come true without you.

From Nobel Peace Prize acceptance speech, 2011 | Tawakkol Karman, *Yemeni journalist, politician and activist* (b.1979)

If I might thus speak to girls and women everywhere, I would issue them this simple invitation: my sisters, my daughters, my friends, find your voices!

From Nobel Peace Prize acceptance speech, 2011 | Ellen Johnson Sirleaf, *President of Liberia, first female head of state in an African country and joint recipient with Karman of the Nobel Peace Prize* (b.1938)

Today is indeed an historic occasion when as first chair-in-office woman I hand over to another woman chair-in-office, your Prime Minister, Julia Gillard, in the presence of a woman head of the Commonwealth, Her Majesty the Queen of England.

From speech at the Commonwealth Heads of Government meeting in Perth, 28 October 2011 | Kamla Persad-Bissessar, *politician, Trinidad and Tobago* (b.1952)

I know people are not used to seeing confident, educated, happy, chunky African American girls, and I don't care. They're just going to have to get used to it.

Precious Lee, *fashion model* (b.1989)

There is no handbook for incoming First Ladies of the United States. It's not technically a job, nor is it an official government title. It comes with no salary and no spelled-out set of obligations. It's a strange kind of sidecar to the presidency, a seat that by the time I came to it had been occupied by more than forty-three different women, each of whom had done it her own way...

I understood already that I'd be measured by a different yardstick. As the only African American First Lady to set foot in the White House, I was 'other' almost by default. If there was a presumed grace assigned to my white predecessors, I knew it wasn't likely to be the same for me. I'd learned through the campaign stumbles that I had to be better, faster, smarter, and stronger than ever. My grace would need to be earned. I worried that many Americans wouldn't see themselves reflected in me, or that they wouldn't relate to my journey. I wouldn't have the luxury of settling into my new role slowly before being judged. And when it came to judgement, I was as vulnerable as ever to the unfounded fears and racial stereotypes that lay just beneath the surface of the public consciousness, ready to be stirred up by rumor and innuendo.

I was humbled and excited to be First Lady, but not for one second did I think I'd be sliding into some glamorous, easy role. Nobody who has the words 'first' and 'Black' attached to them ever would. I stood at the foot of the mountain, knowing I'd need to climb my way into favor.

For me, it revived an old internal call-and-response, one that tracked all the way back to high school, when I'd shown up at Whitney Young [high school] and found myself suddenly gripped by doubt. Confidence, I'd learned then, sometimes needs to be called from within. I've repeated the same words to myself now, through many climbs.

Am I good enough? Yes I am.

From *Becoming*, 2018 | Michelle Obama (b.1964)

On the campaign, I would often say when we fight, we win. But here's the thing, here's the thing, sometimes the fight takes a while. That doesn't mean we won't win. That doesn't mean we won't win. The important thing is don't ever give up. Don't ever give up. Don't ever stop trying to make the world a better place. You have power. You have power. And don't you ever listen when anyone tells you something is impossible because it has never been done before.

You have the capacity to do extraordinary good in the world. And so to everyone who is watching, do not despair. This is not a time to throw up our hands. This is a time to roll up our sleeves. This is a time to organize, to mobilize, and to stay engaged for the sake of freedom and justice and the future that we all know we can build together. Look, many of you know I started out as a prosecutor and throughout my career I saw people at some of the worst times in their lives. People who had suffered great harm and great pain, and yet found within themselves the strength and the courage and the resolve to take the stand, to take a stand, to fight for justice, to fight for themselves, to fight for others. So let their courage be our inspiration. Let their determination be our charge. And I'll close with this. There's an adage a historian once called a law of history, true of every society across the ages. The adage is, only when it is dark enough can you see the stars.

From concession speech, 6 November 2024, after losing the contest to become America's first female president | Kamala Harris (b. 1964)

If you have made mistakes, even serious mistakes, there is always another chance for you. And supposing you have tried and failed again and again, you may have a fresh start any moment you choose, for this thing we call 'failure' is not the falling down, but the staying down.

Mary Pickford (1892–1979)

Chapter 2

FAMILY

FAMILY

I may hate her, but that's not all. I ... love her too. After all, as the story goes, she's my mother

Diary entry, 26 December 1958 | Sylvia Plath (1932–1963)

In search of my mother's garden, I found my own.

Alice Walker (b.1944)

Hold dear to your parents, because it is a scary and confusing world without them.

Emily Dickinson (1830–1886)

My dearest Fanny,
You are inimitable, irresistible. You are the delight of my Life. Such Letters, such entertaining Letters as you have lately sent! – Such a description of your queer little heart! – Such a lovely display of what Imagination does – You are worth your weight in Gold, or even in the new Silver Coinage. – I cannot express to you what I have felt in reading your history of yourself, how full of Pity & Concern & Admiration & Amusement I have been. You are the Paragon of all that is Silly & Sensible, common-place & eccentric, Sad & Lively, Provoking & Interesting. – Who can keep pace with the fluctuations of your Fancy, the Capprizios of your Taste, the Contradictions of

your Feelings! – You are so odd! – & all the time, so perfectly natural – so peculiar in yourself, & yet so like everybody else! – It is very, very gratifying to me to know you so intimately. You can hardly think what a pleasure it is to me, to have such thorough pictures of your Heart. – Oh! What a loss it will be, when you are married. You are too agreeable in your single state, too agreeable as a Neice [sic]. I shall hate you when your delicious play of mind is all settled down into conjugal and maternal affections.

Jane Austen (1775 –1817) to her niece Fanny Knight, 20 February 1817

My dearest Fanny,
I have just read your letter for the third time, and thank you most sincerely for every kind expression to myself, and still more warmly for your praises of her who I believe was better known to you than any human being besides myself. Nothing of the sort could have been more gratifying to me than the manner in which you write of her, and if the dear angel is conscious of what passes here, and is not above all earthly feelings, she may perhaps receive pleasure in being so mourned. Had she been the survivor I can fancy her speaking of you in almost the same terms. There are certainly many points of strong resemblance in your characters; in your intimate acquaintance with each other, and your mutual strong affection, you were counterparts.

Cassandra Austen (1773–1845) to her niece Fanny Knight after the death of her sister Jane, 29 July 1817

I think my life began with waking up and loving my mother's face.

From *Daniel Deronda*, 1876 | George Eliot (1819–1880)

Elinor, this eldest daughter whose advice was so effectual, possessed a strength of understanding, and coolness of judgement, which qualified her, though only nineteen, to be the counsellor of her mother, and enabled her frequently to counteract, to the advantage of them all, that eagerness of mind in Mrs Dashwood which must generally have led to imprudence. She had an excellent heart; – her disposition was affectionate, and her feelings were strong; but she knew how to govern them: it was a knowledge which her mother had yet to learn, and which one of her sisters had resolved never to be taught.

From *Sense and Sensibility*, 1811 | Jane Austen (1775–1817)

...all the evil and good of their earliest years could be gone over again, and every former united pain and pleasure retraced with the fondest recollections. An advantage this, a strengthener of love, in which even the conjugal tie is beneath the fraternal. Children of the same family, the same blood, with the same first associations and habits, have some means of enjoyment in their power, which no subsequent connection can supply...

From *Mansfield Park*, 1814 | Jane Austen (1776–1817)

From *Goblin Market*

Days, weeks, months, years
Afterwards, when both were wives
With children of their own:
Their mother-hearts beset with fears,
Their lives bound up in tender lives;
Laura would call the little ones

And tell them of her early prime,
Those pleasant days long gone
Of not-returning time: ...
Would tell them how her sister stood
In deadly peril to do her good,
And win the fiery antidote:
Then joining hands to little hands
Would bid them cling together,
'For there is no friend like a sister
In calm or stormy weather:
To cheer one on the tedious way,
To fetch one if one goes astray,
To lift one if one totters down,
To strengthen while one stands.

Christina Rossetti (1830–1894)

At home. Sew, read & write a little. Nan's [her sister's] birthday on the 16th (48). The best woman I know, always reasonable, just, kind & forgiving. A heavenly temper & a tender heart. A good sister to me all these years in spite of the utter unlikeness of our tastes, temperaments & lives. If we did not love one another so well we never could get on at all. As it is I am a trial to her & she to me sometimes, our views are so different. Dear, loving soul. God bless & keep her long to be our comfort.

Diary entry, March 1879 | Louisa May Alcott (1832–1888)

Sisters are a shield against life's cruel adversity.

Nancy Mitford (1904–1973)

My sister and I were very different, which is often true of sisters. I see now that talking a lot, like writing for me, was a way to validate herself in a family that rarely listened. I am such a lover of silence, I used to joke, it will no doubt be a pleasure to be dead.

Diary entry, April 1993, from *Gathering Blossoms Under Fire*, 2022 | Alice Walker (b.1944)

'Do not urge me to leave you or to return from following you. For where you go I will go, and where you lodge I will lodge. Your people shall be my people, and your God my God. Where you die I will die, and there will I be buried. May the Lord do so to me and more also if anything but death parts me from you.'

Ruth from *The Bible*, Book of Ruth 1:16–17 to her mother-in-law Naomi

Every Lunar New Year, my grandmother is up before the first light breaks across the sky. First, she heads downstairs to burn offerings at the side of the road for our ancestors. Then she is at the flower market for all the new year essentials - narcissus plants resting in water, a handful of mandarins. She takes the double-decker bus home and hauls her purchases up the five flights of stairs in our walk-up building, all by herself, with the kind of inhuman strength only grandmothers possess.

From *The Impossible City: A Hong Kong Memoir* 2022 | Karen Cheung

My paternal grandmother, Grandma Jane, was hardly a model of convention either, a novelist, whose heroines dared to challenge narrow ideas of propriety and whose own indomitable spirit overcame many of the barriers that might have circumscribed her life. She survived a car crash at 90, correcting the state trooper who sought to comfort her as she was being cut from the wreckage for mistakenly asking what an old lady 'of 91' was doing driving on her own in such icy Chicago weather, and confounding the surgeons who first predicted she would die from her injuries, then that she would never walk again. A couple of years later, she marched unaided into a starchy restaurant, where an overattentive waiter fussed around her, addressing his questions to me as if she might be too enfeebled by age to answer for herself. Jane leaned across the table and in a sibilant stage whisper wondered aloud, 'What do you think this nice young man would do if I asked him to fuck off?'

From *Amortality: The Pleasures and Perils of Living Agelessly*, 2011 | Catherine Mayer (b.1961)

She could hardly breathe. Joy, release, triumph enfolded her.

'I don't think you know how fond I am of you,' she said.

'Perhaps I do.'

Hicks had turned the horse again; the dog cart was approaching them, its lamps faint and small beside the great lights of the passing motor-cars. In another moment this little interlude of tenderness would be over.

'By the way,' he added, 'that reminds me.' He fumbled in his waistcoat pocket and brought out a little box wrapped in tissue paper. 'I brought a little present for you too.'

'For me?'

'Yes. I want you to have it. You will know why. Good-bye. Merry Christmas to you.'

He took her hand, smiled, then very gravely stooped and kissed her soft wrinkled cheek and was off, out of the gate. She heard him call to Hicks; she saw the moving lights stop still; he climbed into the cart; he shook the reins, then the hoofs were off again, trot-trotting away from her into the starlight.

She put her hand to her face and touched it gently. He had never kissed her before. She had not dreamed of it. With trembling hands she began to undo her Christmas present. The paper contained a small brown case lined with white velvet, and on the velvet lay the brooch, a spray of emeralds, diamonds and rubies, which he bought for Muriel when Midge was born. He had slipped into the lid a little card on which he had written, 'For Midge's Granny, in gratitude.'

'I want you to have it,' he had said. 'You will know why.' She knew why.

She had tried to give to Midge the protective love which her mother could not give. He had recognised her endeavour and was grateful. He had given her the brooch he bought for Muriel, and he had kissed her.

She knew now where she stood with him, and she was happy. Her jealousy and pain were taken from her. Whatever problems and griefs still lay before her - and she had no doubt that they would still be many - she realised that her long years of patient loyalty and service had at least brought this difficult and strange relationship through to triumphant confidence and love.

From *South Riding*, 1936 | Winifred Holtby (1898–1935)

Ninety-nine percent of the time humans have lived on this planet we've lived in tribes, groups of 12 to 36 people. Only during times of war, or what we have now, which is the psychological equivalent of war, does the nuclear family prevail, because it's the most mobile unit that can ensure the survival of the species. But for the full flowering of the human spirit we need groups, tribes.

Margaret Mead, *cultural anthropologist* (1901–1978)

Being a housewife and a mother is the biggest job in the world, but if it doesn't interest you, don't do it... I would have made a terrible parent. The first time my child didn't do what I wanted, I'd kill him.

Katherine Hepburn (1907–2003)

Some are kissing mothers and some are scolding mothers, but it is love just the same, and most mothers kiss and scold together.

From *To My Daughter, With Love*, 1967 | Pearl S. Buck (1892–1973)

When Vivi reached out her hand to Sidda, she took it. Their hands rested on the swing between them. At the same moment, each of them looked down and noticed the similarity of their hands coloring, the shape of their fingers, the veins that carried their Ya-Ya blood through their female bodies.

'Oh, my,' Vivi sighed.

'Oh, my,' Sidda echoed.

With those few sounds, it was as though mother and daughter exchanged the same breath. Then, without a word, they began to push against the ground with their feet, so that the swing began to rock ever so gently. Nothing rambunctious, just a smooth swaying, as if the swing were a cradle holding both mother and daughter, two separate and equal planets tumbling through space one night in late autumn.

From *Divine Secrets of the Ya-Ya Sisterhood*, 1996 | Rebecca Wells (b.1952)

From *My Mother*

Who fed me from her gentle breast,
And hushed me in her arms to rest,
And on my cheek sweet kisses prest?
My Mother.

When sleep forsook my open eye,
Who was it sung sweet hushaby,
And rocked me that I should not cry?
My Mother.

Who sat and watched my infant head,
When sleeping on my cradle bed,
And tears of sweet affection shed?
My Mother.

When pain and sickness made me cry,
Who gazed upon my heavy eye,
And wept, for fear that I should die?
My Mother.

Who dressed my doll in clothes so gay,
And fondly taught me how to play,
And minded all I had to say?
My Mother.

Who ran to help me when I fell,
And would some pretty story tell,
Or kiss the place to make it well?
My Mother.

Who taught my infant lips to pray,
And love God's holy book and day,
And walk in wisdom's pleasant way?
My Mother.

And can I ever cease to be
Affectionate and kind to thee,
Who was so very kind to me,
My Mother?

Ah no! the thought I cannot bear,
And if God please my life to spare,
I hope I shall reward thy care,
My Mother.

When thou art feeble, old, and grey,
My healthy arm shall be thy stay,
And I will soothe thy pains away,
My Mother.

And when I see thee hang thy head,
'Twill be my turn to watch thy bed,
And tears of sweet affection shed,
My Mother.

For could our Father in the skies
Look down with pleased or loving eyes,
If ever I could dare despise,
My Mother.

Ann Taylor (1783–1824)

'How I wish I were a boy!' Mother caught me saying this aloud one day, and promptly told me that this was a wicked thought. She did not go on to give a reason, but merely insisted that it was splendid to be a girl, and with such exuberant enthusiasm that I was quite convinced.

From *A London Child of the Seventies*, 1934 | Mary 'Molly' Hughes (1866–1956)

I long to hear if you be grown big yet and if you keep your meat well. I hope you will grow stronger and be better and better with every child till all the twenty be born that you used to wish for...

My sister writes me word that you look very well. I pray God it may continue. There is nothing so good for you and the child both as to be merry, so I entreat you let not anything that falls out disquiet and vex you for it never alters the matter that troubles us and does much displease and dishonour God.

Margaret, Countess of Wemyss (1659–1705) to her pregnant daughter Anne, 1695

...my mother and I watched The Sound of Music. Because of the commercials, it took more than four hours. Julie Andrews sang about how she must have done something good in her youth or childhood, and my mother sang along. She said she had probably done something good in my childhood, because I had turned out so well.

From *The Idiot*, 2017 | Elif Batuman (b.1977)

Whenever I feel myself inferior to everything about me, threatened by my own mediocrity, frightened by the discovery that a muscle is losing its strength, a desire its power, or a pain the keen edge of its bite, I can still hold up my head and say to myself... 'I am the daughter of a woman who, in a mean, close-fisted, confined little place, opened her village home to stray cats, tramps, and pregnant servant girls... I am the daughter of a woman who bent her head, trembling, between the blades of a cactus, her wrinkled face full of ecstasy over the promise of a flower, a woman who herself never ceased to flower, untiringly, during three quarters of a century.'

From *Earthly Paradise*, 1953 | Colette (1873–1954)

I have now returned from the Bath to my own house in the country, where I thank God I find my little one well, though I much feared it, for I have found your ladyship's words true about the [wet] nurse had for her, for she hath been one of the unhealthfullest women that I think I ever saw, and so extremely troubled with toothache and rheums and swelling in her face as could be, and one night she fell very ill, and was taken like an ague, so as she had but little milk left, and so I was enforced to send for the next woman that was by to give my child suck, whom hath continued with her ever since, and I thank God the child agrees so well with her milk as can be, so I mean not to change her any more. It is a miracle to me that the child should prosper so well, considering the change of her milk. She is but a little one, I confess, but a livelier and merrier thing was there never seen.

Anne Clifford (1590–1656) to her mother, 1614

We were bred tenderly, for my mother naturally did strive to please and delight her children, not to cross and torment them, terrifying them with threats, or lashing them with slavish whips; but instead of threats, reason was used to persuade us, and instead of lashes, the deformity of vice was discovered, and the graces and virtues were presented unto us.

From *A True Relation of My Birth, Breeding, and Life*, 1656 | Margaret Cavendish, Duchess of Newcastle (1623–1673)

My little girl begins to suck so manfully that her father reckons saucily on her writing the second part of the R[igh]ts of Woman.

Mary Wollstonecraft (1759–1797) to Ruth Barlow, 20 May 1794

My heart abounded with joy and gratitude, when my dear little girl was born, perfect and lovely. Words are not equal to express my feelings, for I was most mercifully dealt with, my soul was so quiet, and so much supported.

Diary entry, 1803 | Elizabeth Fry, *prison reformer* (1780–1845)

Your news is most welcome on every account – a girl is better than a boy as you have plenty of the latter and there is less trouble and expense in setting up the former forward in the world, let alone their being often greater comfort to parents, whereby I mean no reflection however.

Maria Josefa Stanley (1771–1863) to her son, 1842

Increasingly, motherhood comes to seem to me not a condition but a job, the work of certain periods, which begin and end and outside which I am free. My daughter is more and more a part of this freedom, something new that is being added, drop by daily drop, to the sum of what I am. We are an admixture, an experiment. I don't yet know what effect her presence will have on my life, but its claim is more profound, more unnerving than was the mere work of looking after her. For the first year of her life work and love were bound together, fiercely, painfully. Now it is as if a relationship has untethered itself and been let loose in our house. A storm of association rages around her, and at first I find this change relieving, as if I had been speaking a foreign language all this time and could at last revert to my native tongue. But in fact, she has not been waiting all this time merely to speak to me: her ability to relate to other people has grown, like tentacles, out of the body of what she has already become. When finally we are able to converse, I find her decided, fully formed, already beyond the reach of persuasion. My relationship with her is like my relationship with anybody: it takes the form of a search for oneness, a oneness lost but haunting with the possibility of its recapture. It is incredible to me – who remembers that oneness, the image on the screen of her two-inch-long body lying there in my darkness, as if it were yesterday, as if it were still there – that our joinedness is for her such a distant state.

From *A Life's Work: On Becoming a Mother*, 2001 | Rachel Cusk (b.1967)

Changing ideas in the outer world were also reflected in the relationship between husband and wife. Marriage was becoming more of a partnership. The man of the house was no longer absolved of all further responsibility when he had brought his week's wages home; he was made to feel that he had an interest in the management of the home and the bringing up of the children. A good, steady husband who could be depended upon was encouraged to keep part of his wages, out of which he paid the rent, bought the pig's food, and often the family footwear. He would sweep the path, chop the wood and fetch water from the well.

'So you be takin' a turn at 'ooman's work?' the older men would say teasingly, and the older women had plenty to say about the lazy, good-for-nothing wenches of these days; but the good example was not lost; the better-natured among the older men began to do odd jobs about their homes, and though, at first, their wives would tell them to 'keep out o' th' road', and say that they could do it themselves in half the time, they soon learned to appreciate it, then to expect it.

From *Larkrise to Candleford*, 1945 | Flora Thompson, *writing about the late nineteenth century* (1876–1947)

There is nothing in this world quite so wonderful as the faith a child has in one they love.

Martha Jane Canary, 'Calamity Jane', (1852–1903) to her daughter, 30 May 1882

Dear Mother, – Into your Christmas stocking I have put my 'first-born,' knowing that you will accept it with all its faults (for grandmothers are always kind), and look upon it merely as an earnest of what I may yet do; for, with so much to cheer me on, I hope to pass in time from fairies and fables to men and realities.

Whatever beauty of poetry is to be found in my little book is owing to your interest in and encouragement of all my efforts from the first to the last; and if ever I do anything to be proud of, my greatest happiness will be that I can thank you for that, as I may do for all the good that is in me; and I shall be content to write if it gives you pleasure.

Louisa May Alcott (1832–1888), to her mother, with a copy of her first book, *Flower Fables*, 25 December 1815

Madame my very dear mother,
I cannot express how touched I am by the kindness Your Majesty has shown me, and I can swear to you that I have not received one of your dear letters without having the tears come to my eyes because I am separated from so kind and loving a mother, and although I am very well situated here, I still ardently wish I could see my dear and very dear family for a moment at least...

Marie Antoinette (1755–1793), ***aged fifteen and newly married to the Dauphin of France,*** **to her mother, 12 July 1770**

Well, Georgy, this marriage is – yes, I will speak well of it, after all; for when I can stop and think long enough to discriminate my head from my heels, I must say that I think myself a fortunate woman both in husband and children. My children I would not change for all the ease, leisure and pleasure that I could have without them. They are money on interest whose value will be constantly increasing.

Harriet Beecher Stowe (1811–1896) to Georgiana May, 21 June 1832

What a delicate office is that of a mother! How wary should be her footsteps, how spotless her example, how uniform her patience, how extensive her knowledge of the human heart, how great her skill in using that knowledge, by the most vigilant and strenuous application of it in every variety of occurring circumstances, to enlighten the understanding and reform the heart! ...Oh that a constant sense of the importance and responsibility of this station may rest upon me! that grace may be given faithfully to discharge its difficult duties.

Susan Huntington (1781–1813)

I already begin to be devoured with expectation. I hope for no consolation but from your letters; and yet I know they will only make me sigh still more deeply. In short, my dear child, I live but for you. Would I loved God with equal fervour!

Madame de Sévigné (1626–1696) to her daughter, 5 October 1673

One thing I had learned from watching chimpanzees with their infants is that having a child should be fun.

Jane Goodall, *primatologist* (b.1934)

I have been playing and laughing with the little girl so long, that I cannot take up my pen to address you without emotion. Pressing her to my bosom, she looked so like you... every book seemed to vibrate to the touch, and I began to think that there was something in the assertion of man and wife being one...

Mary Wollstonecraft (1759–1797) to Gilbert Imlay, 25 September 1794

To My Dear Children

This book by any yet unread,
I leave for you when I am dead,
That being gone, you here may find
What was your living mother's mind.
Make use of what I leave in Love,
And God shall bless you from above.

Anne Bradstreet (1612–1672)

...the creature who wanted us to be invulnerable was herself too tender, too delicate, too much gifted for suffering. She who had voluntarily accustomed us to be undemonstrative, would no doubt have wished, without confessing it, to have us embrace and cajole her more...

Like a great many children, we were probably selfish and insensitive to shades of feeling. Just the same we perceived the charm, the restrained tenderness and the hidden grace of her we call - in the first line of our letters spotted with ink, stupid little letters which, tied up with confectioners' ribbons, Marie kept until her death - 'Darling Mé,' 'My sweet darling,' 'My sweet,' or else, most often, 'Sweet Mé.'

Sweet, too sweet 'Mé', who could hardly be heard, who spoke to us almost timidly, who wanted to be neither feared nor respected nor admired... Sweet Mé who, along the years, neglected completely to apprise us that she was not a mother like every other mother, nor a professor crushed under daily tasks, but an exceptional human being, an illustrious woman.

From *Madame Curie*, 1937 | Eva Curie (1904–2007)

Precepts for the guidance of a daughter

Wash your hands.
When you have washed them, hold a book in them.
Diminish your calves.
Pluck your arms...
Get up early, but not too early...

Mrs Gaskell (1810–1865)

As very little children I accustomed them to playing in the dark. Many a game of hide and seek have I had with them in [a] room bordered by [a] dressing-room and two closets, and admitting of all kinds of surprises. They were never afraid of any kind of insect, would handle beetles, spiders, earwigs, etcetera, with pleasure, and were much amused if anyone was afraid of them.

Anna Sewell has this day completed her ninth year, and is in many respects a delight and comfort to her mother, who, that she may be able to test her progress from year to year, wished now to write a short account of her attainments in her learning, and of the qualities of her mind, etcetera...

Mary Sewell (1792–1894), on her children Anna (author of *Black Beauty*) and Philip

I have had so much more than I deserve, and now I am quite bewildered and overpowered. It is so good to feel that one is loved – the only real riches in the world, and I am very happy in that. I think my soul came to me quite suddenly, when I was about eleven years old, and all at once I realised how precious you were to me – since then have we not been growing nearer and nearer? When we go to the next world I hope St. Peter will not know which is which.

Freya Stark (1893–1993) to her mother, 1 February 1914

1600 Pennsylvania Avenue [The White House]
Washington, D C
Xmas Eve 1935
Darling Anna,
Perhaps I needed to have you away this Xmas to realize just how much it means to have you & so I think I'll try to tell you in these few minutes before dinner just how much I miss you. The dogs & I have

felt sad every time we passed your door, it was very hard to decorate the tree or get things distributed at the afternoon party without you and I dread dinner tomorrow night for so many of your friends will miss you & if anyone says much I shall weep for I've had a queer feeling in my throat whenever I thought of you.

Eleanor Roosevelt (1884–1962) to her daughter Anna, 24 December 1935

There is a photograph I have kept of my mother in her late twenties. She is sitting on a rock at a picnic with friends. Her hair is wet because she's just had a swim. There is a kind of introspection in her expression that I now relate to the very best of her. I can see that she is close to herself in this random moment. I'm not sure that I thought her introspection was the best of her when I was a child and teenager. What do we need dreamy mothers for? We do not want mothers who gaze beyond us, longing to be elsewhere. We need her to be of this world, lively, capable, entirely present to our needs...

The older I get, the more of my mother I see in myself. The more opposite my life and thinking grow from hers, the more of her I hear in my voice, see in my facial expressions, feel in the emotional reactions I have come to recognize as my own. It is almost as if in extending myself, the circle closes in to completion. She was my first and my most lasting model. To say her image is not still a touchstone in my life - and mine in hers - would be another lie. I am tired of lies.

From *My Mother/My Self*, 1977 | Nancy Friday (1933–2017)

It is unbelievable to me now to think I did not know them last week. 'Why, you look just like your mother!' a woman said to me recently. I thought she meant I was wearing my mother's tight, anxious look. But she was thinking of something else. 'The last time I saw her,' this woman went on, 'your mother bid a grand slam. It was four o'clock in the morning, and she made it!'...

I said in the first chapter of this book that I'd often wished my mother had had my life. Hubris again, snidely competitive, and damned impertinent too. I don't think she'd want it. The more I grow away from her and define myself, the more I see in her this other person she was before she became Nancy Friday's mother. That is the magic: not that we can ever recreate that nirvana of love that may or may not have existed between us as mother-and-child, but that once we have separated we can give each other life, extra life, each out of the abundance of our own.

Recognizing the woman who can bid a grand slam at four in the morning when the rest of the world is asleep, I sleep better myself. Now that I have granted her the right to have run off with my father at seventeen because she was a sexual adventuress at heart – and not because it was some atypical bit of foolishness which had nothing to do with her true character at all – I can be proud of that part of myself that is a sexual woman too.

From *My Mother/My Self*, 1977 | Nancy Friday (1933–2017)

A secret cord that can't be cut binds us to the bodies of our mothers: there is no way to detach ourselves, or at least I've never managed to. It's impossible to go back inside her; it's hard to move past her shadow.

So I quickly put many other bodies between hers and mine – bodies with which I could be the boss, quarrel, make love, appear wise or foolish – constructing a world alien to hers. I wanted her to feel uneasy if she merely looked in on it: that happened often, and she escaped in silence.

Over the years, she withdrew. She got smaller, she lost beauty and cleverness, she stopped asserting her own superiority in everything, her words no longer had weight.

For a while I felt free. Then people began to say things like, 'You laugh like your mother, you're stubborn like your mother, you have your mother's hands.' One morning I looked at myself in the mirror and I recognised her: she was there, in my body. And to my surprise it began to bother me less and less; slowly I discovered her in my gestures, in a particular way of showing or controlling feelings, in my voice. If it was impossible to go back inside my mother, it was very possible that she had been inside me since birth, and that she could be found inside me even when I fought to escape her – even when I thought I was free of her.

From the *Guardian*, 25 August 1981 | Elena Ferrante (b.1943), translated by Ann Goldstein

Buckingham Palace

My own darling Child,

Your dear little note reached me just as we were sitting down to dinner, and gave us both the greatest pleasure. We missed you much. The object for which so much had been going on had disappeared, the object of our tenderest solicitude for 17 years is now in other but truly safe and loving hands.

This has been a very trying day for you, my dearest child – and you behaved excessively well so that you have only added to the love and affection that so many bear to you. It is very solemn act, the most important and solemn in every one's life, but much much more so in a woman's than a man's...

Queen Victoria (1819–1901) to 'Vicky', the Princess Royal, who had been married earlier that day, 25 January 1858

Berlin
Dear Mama, I did not think you would miss me as you do, I was often such a plague to you; but sweet is the thought that one is missed by those whom one loves so passionately so intensely as I love Papa and you, and the dear children and the whole of England. It pains me that you should still be sad. If you knew how much nearer I feel drawn to you, my beloved parents, instead of feeling myself cut off from you, I feel that I am serving you both and proving my deep gratitude to you, in doing my duty here and in imitating your great and glorious example. I may I hope be of real use to you. How happy that would make me.

'Vicky', the Princess Royal (1840–1901) to Queen Victoria, 15 February 1858

Osborne
In your letter of the 16th you allude to your love for me, and your fearing you had not shown it always well, formerly, and you hope that I never doubted your affection for me. Doubt your real affection and your love, I did not, dearest child – but you did all you could to make me doubt it, for a more insubordinate and unequal-tempered child and girl I think I never saw! I must say so, honestly, now, dear. The tone you used to me, you know, shocked all who heard you, and if we had not made you feel that – you might have been very unhappy and made your husband very unhappy. The trouble you gave us all – was indeed very great. Comparatively speaking, we have none whatever with the others. You and Bertie (in very different ways) were indeed great difficulties. But life – life with its bright and its dark sides, its joys and its trials, as you learn it now, has done and will do what I believe nothing else could or would. And so it always is! I am very curious to know whether I shall find some of the old tricks of former times in you? The standing on one leg, the violent laughing – the cramming in eating, the waddling in walking...

Queen Victoria (1819–1901) to 'Vicky', the Princess Royal, 28 July 1858

Windsor Castle
My beloved child, these lines are to wish you heartily and warmly joy of your 20th birthday – an important age – though married nearly three years and with two children it seems but of little consequence. Still to bid adieu to one's 'teens' is a serious thing! May every earthly blessing and happiness be in store for you for many and many years – and your beloved husband and dear children be spared to you through a long and happy life! Our gifts will I trust please you.

Last year we had the happiness of having you here; how I wish it could be so now again! But as we cannot embrace you, and celebrate the day in person – we must and shall do so in thought.

Far or near, my love and affection and solicitude will ever be the same, my beloved child.

God bless you. Ever your devoted Mama.

Queen Victoria (1819–1901) to 'Vicky', the Princess Royal, 17 November 1860

Don't blame your parents too much! We all had parents. There is only one way of escaping from their influence and that is by going into the matter with yourself – examining yourself and making perfectly sure of their share.

It can be done. One is NEVER free until one has done blaming somebody or praising somebody for what is bad & good in one. ...Dont [sic] think I underestimate the enormous power that parents can have. I dont. Its staggering – its titanic. After all they are real giants while we are only table high & they act accordingly. But like everything else in Life – I mean all the suffering, however great – we have to get over it, to cease from harking back to it, to grin & bear it & to hide our wounds. More than that and far more true is we have to find the gift in it. We cant afford to waste such an expenditure of feeling; we have to learn from it – and we *do*, I most deeply believe, come to be thankful for it.

Katherine Mansfield (1888–1923) to Dorothy Brett, 1 March 1921

Did I mock the dreamer in my mother and then insult her for having no dreams?

From *The Cost of Living*, 2018 | Deborah Levy (b.1959)

Love did find its way through the on and off war between myself and my mother. The poet Audre Lorde said it best: 'I am a reflection of my mother's secret poetry as well as of her hidden angers.' She sent me a postcard from Johannesburg in 1992... My mother had made a biro'd X on the front of the postcard and written, X is where I am. She seems to have been located in a neighbourhood somewhere beyond a big flyover, near a telephone tower and a skyscraper. It is this X that touches me most now, her hand holding the biro, pressing it into the postcard, marking where she is so that I can find her.

From *The Cost of Living*, 2018 | Deborah Levy (b.1959)

Before her kidney-shaped dressing table with its triple mirrors, its side drawers stuffed with her nylons, the central one with her palette of Revlon blue eyeshadow, her gold tubes of Max Factor lipsticks and her small bottle of Elizabeth Arden Blue Grass scent, I watched my mother become a person who had an existence out in the world, not just inside the house. She made me realise that inner identity is not fixed. That she could be something or, more worryingly someone, apart from a mother.

From *The Thoughtful Dresser*, 2009 | Linda Grant (b.1951)

I think I'm taking back a part of myself from my mother's shadow. Because she shared everything, space, time, resources, I feel I must. But, as Jean pointed out, you cannot share solitude. Especially not working solitude. My mother did the kind of work that could tolerate interruptions - & eight children certainly primed her to be interrupted. She was a storyteller, not a novelist. I have wanted to emulate her wonderful generosity. And I've wanted to take care of others as she did. But the minute I feel I have to do it I begin to resent the people. They begin to grate on me. Get on my nerves. I find fault with them. And then I am upset with myself for not being better.

Well, I am no better than I am.

Diary entry, 4 December 1996, from *Gathering Blossoms Under Fire* | Alice Walker (b.1944)

From *Black Mother Woman*

But I have peeled away your anger
down to the core of love
and look, mother
I Am
a dark temple where your true spirit rises.

***A Land Where Other People Live*, 1972 | Audre Lorde (1934–1992)**

Her [her mother's] illness had quite broken the shell of her prejudices and her pretensions: perhaps because she no longer needed these defences. No question of renunciation or sacrifice any more: her first duty was to get better and so to look after herself; giving herself up to her own wishes and her own pleasures with no holding back, she was at last freed from resentment. Her restored beauty and her recovered smile expressed her inner harmony and, on this death-bed, a kind of happiness.

From *A Very Easy Death*, 1964 | Simone de Beauvoir (1908–1986)

What touched our hearts that day was the way she [mother] noticed the slightest agreeable sensation: it was as though, at the age of seventy-eight, she were waking afresh to the miracle of living. While the nurse was settling her pillows the metal of a tube touched her thigh – 'It's cool! How pleasant!' She breathed in the smell of eau-de-Cologne and talcum powder – 'How good it smells.' She had the bunches of flowers and the plants arranged on her wheeled table. 'The little red roses come from Meyrignac. At Meyrignac there are roses still.' She asked us to raise the curtain that was covering the window and she looked at the golden leaves of the trees. 'How lovely! I shouldn't see that from my flat!' She smiled. And both of us, my sister and I, had the same thought: it was that same smile that had dazzled us when we were little children, the radiant smile of a young woman. Where had it been between then and now?

From *A Very Easy Death*, 1964 | Simone de Beauvoir (1908–1986)

My only, dearest, beloved Mamotschka! This is the end. Today, at dark, your Lanka will no longer be alive. My consolation and hope is my little Irka [her daughter] who, thank God, has no notion of what is happening around her. Mamico, you were to me the best mother on earth. You have done to me whatever is possible to do, and I thank you. Forgive me my death, forgive me every offence which you have suffered from me, every ugly word; I beg you, I implore you, crown your work as a mother and keep strong!!!

Liana Berkowitz (1923–1943) to her mother from Plötzensee Prison (*a resistance fighter, she was executed later the same day*), 5 August 1943

february 13, 1980

twenty-one years of my life you have been
the lost color in my eye, my secret blindness,
all my seeings turn grey with your going.
mother, I have worn your name like a shield.
it has torn but protected me all these years,
now even your absence comes of age.
i put on a dress called woman for this day
but I am not grown away from you
whatever I say.

Lucille Clifton (1936–2010)

'Now you understand my meaning,' said my mother triumphantly.

I smiled.

And really, I did understand finally. Not what she had just said. But what had been true all along.

I saw what I had been fighting for: It was for me, a scared child, who had run away a long time ago to what I had imagined was a safer place. And hiding in this place, behind my invisible barriers, I knew what lay on the other side: Her side attacks. Her secret weapons. Her uncanny ability to find my weakest spots. But in the brief instant that I had peered over the barriers I could finally see what was really there: an old woman, a wok for her armor, a knitting needle for her sword, getting a little crabby as she waited patiently for her daughter to invite her in.

From *The Joy Luck Club*, 1989 | Amy Tan (b.1952)

My mother was very happy as I sat by her. But I think she knew that death was near, for she said strange things to me – things touching the emotions she would never have dared say otherwise, for affection between parents and children was never shown among my people. She called me 'my daughter' – a thing she had never said before in her life.

'I don't know how I could of lived till now if it hadn't been for you,' she said once, as if the words were wrung from her.

Once in the middle of the night she woke me to say: 'Promise me you'll go on an' git a better edjication.' Her hand closed upon mine, steady and strong, as if asking for a pledge.

From *Daughter of Earth*, 1929 | Agnes Smedley, *American journalist and activist for Indian independence and the Chinese Communist Revolution* (1892–1950)

I know I will spend the next years figuring out what her life has left in me.

I realize that I've always been more touched by old people than by children. It's the talent and hopes locked up in a failing body that gets to me; a poignant contrast that reminds me of my mother, even when she was strong ...

I'm no longer obsessed, as I was for many years, with the fear that I would end up in a house like that one in Toledo. Now, I'm obsessed instead with the things I could have done for my mother while she was alive, or the things I should have said.

I still don't understand why so many, many years passed before I saw my mother as a person and before I understood that many of the forces in her life are patterns women share. Like a lot of daughters, I suppose I couldn't afford to admit that what had happened to my mother was not all personal or accidental and therefore could happen to me.

'Ruth's Song (Because She Could Not Sing It)', from *Outrageous Acts and Everyday Rebellions*, 1984 | Gloria Steinem (b.1934)

Every act of motherhood contains a dual intent, as the mother holds the child close and prepares it to move away from her, as she supports the child and stands it firmly on its feet, and as she guards it against danger and sends it out across the yard, down by the stream, and across the traffic-crowded highway. Unless a mother can do both - gather her child close and turn her child out toward the world - she will fail in her purpose.

Margaret Mead (1901–1978)

I long to put the experience of fifty years at once into your young lives, to give you at once the key of that treasure chamber every gem of which has cost me tears and struggles and prayers, but you must work for these inward treasures yourselves.

Harriet Beecher Stowe (1811–1896) to her twin daughters, 1861

My mother was a continual source of wisdom and great advice... she taught me that there is always a way around a problem - you've just got to find it. Keep trying doors; one will eventually open. She also taught me to accept failure as part and parcel of life. It's not the opposite of success; it's an integral part of success.

Arianna Huffington (b.1950)

I was proud of my mother. You could put her in a barn and by the way she placed a chair it would become hers. Once I left her I could love her. Distance gave value to all the things around her I had grown up with: the golds and greens and whites of her living room, the flowers, the silver cigarette boxes, the white wicker furniture on the lawn, all were dear to me as they had never been when it had all been mine, when it was all I had. Even her anxiety and shyness that had so upset me as a child were now lovable; they were rallying emotions for all of us. We would follow her into the big comfortable kitchen with our martinis before dinner, as though we didn't want to let her out of our sight, as though to protect her. She would lay elegant tables, prepare wonderful food with an effortlessness I hadn't remembered she had. I began to see talents in my mother I wanted for myself. 'I don't know why we always end up in the kitchen,' she would blush and smile at this new man I had brought home, and I would touch her and say, 'But, Mom, this is where we want to be,' loving her now that I hadn't become like her.

From *My Mother/My Self*, 1977 | Nancy Friday (1933–2017)

How many times have I said in this book that my mother and I are totally different women? Oh, I have acknowledged certain minor virtues I got from her – housekeeping, an easy hostess, etc. But compared to those qualities of hers I have always disliked but taken over anyway – her anxiety and the fear which lies beneath my surface independence – how paltry appeared my 'good' inheritance. I have always thought I had to leave home to reinforce the qualities in myself I wanted... It has taken me the entire writing of this book to acknowledge in my heart that the qualities I am proudest of in myself I learned from her.

From *My Mother/My Self*, 1977 | Nancy Friday (1933–2017)

January 1980
Now, I know you are going to think I hate and despise you for your self-hatred, for your isolation. But I don't. Because in spite of your withdrawal, in spite of your loneliness, you have not only survived, but been beside me in the worst of times when your company meant

everything in the world to me. I just need more than that now, Ma. I have taken and taken from you in terms of needing you to mother me, to be by my side, and I need, now, to take from you two more things: understanding and support for who I am now and my work.

We are Asian American women and the reaction to our identity is what causes the chasms instead of connections. But do you realize, Ma, that I could never have reacted the way I have if you had not provided for me the opportunity to be free of the binds that have held you down, and to be in the process of self-affirmation? Because of your life, because of the physical security you have given me: my education, my full stomach, my clothed and starched back, my piano and dancing lessons – all those gifts you never received – I saw myself as having worth; now I begin to love myself more, see our potential, and fight for just that kind of social change that will affirm me, my race, my sex, my heritage. And while I affirm myself, Ma, I affirm you.

'Letter to Ma', from *This Bridge Called my Back: Writings by Radical Women of Color* | Merle Woo (b.1941)

The square house is screened from the street by a high clipped hedge of laurel. Passing the drive gate you see, at an obtuse angle, and through the branches of a flourishing Wellingtonia, glimpses of slate roof, spacious windows, glass porch with coloured panes. And at once the imagination is engaged .... Here grows something energetic, concentrated, tough, serene; with its own laws and habits; something alarming, oppressive, not altogether to be trusted: nefarious perhaps. Here grows a curious plant with strong roots knotted altogether: a unique specimen. In brief, a family lives here.

From *Invitation to the Waltz*, 1932 | Rosamond Lehmann (1901–1990)

Daughter,
I heard such tidings today that I do perceive (if it be true) the time is very near when Almighty God will prove you; and I am very glad of it for I trust he doth handle you with a good love. I beseech you, agree of His pleasure with a merry heart; and be sure that, without fail, He will not suffer you to perish if you beware to offend Him. I pray you, good daughter, to offer yourself to Him...

But one thing I especially desire you, for the love that you do owe unto God and unto me, to keep your heart with a chaste mind, and your body from all ill and wanton company, [not] thinking or desiring any husband for Christ's passion; neither determine yourself to any manner of living till this troublesome time be past. For I dare make sure that you shall see a very good end, and better than you can desire... And now you shall begin, and by likelihood I shall follow. I set not a rush by it; for when they have done the uttermost they can, then I am sure of the amendment... we never come to the kingdom of Heaven but by troubles. Daughter wheresoever you come, take no pain to send unto me, for if I may, I will send to you,
Your loving mother,
Katherine the Queen

Katherine of Aragon (1485–1536) to Mary Tudor, 1534

From *Rock Me to Sleep*

Backward, turn backward, O Time, in your flight,
Make me a child again just for tonight!
Mother, come back from the echoless shore,
Take me again to your heart as of yore;

Kiss from my forehead the furrows of care,
Smooth the few silver threads out of my hair;
Over my slumbers your loving watch keep;—
Rock me to sleep, mother, - rock me to sleep!

...

Over my heart, in the days that are flown,
No love like mother-love ever has shone;
No other worship abides and endures,—
Faithful, unselfish, and patient like yours:
None like a mother can charm away pain
From the sick soul and the world-weary brain.
Slumber's soft calms o'er my heavy lids creep;—
Rock me to sleep, mother, - rock me to sleep!

Come, let your brown hair, just lighted with gold,
Fall on your shoulders again as of old;
Let it drop over my forehead tonight,
Shading my faint eyes away from the light;
For with its sunny-edged shadows once more
Haply will throng the sweet visions of yore;
Lovingly, softly, its bright billows sweep;—
Rock me to sleep, mother, - rock me to sleep!

Mother, dear mother, the years have been long
Since I last listened your lullaby song:
Sing, then, and unto my soul it shall seem
Womanhood's years have been only a dream.

Clasped to your heart in a loving embrace,
With your light lashes just sweeping my face,
Never hereafter to wake or to weep;—
Rock me to sleep, mother, – rock me to sleep!

Elizabeth Akers Allen (1832–1911)

Chapter 3

FEASTS AND FESTIVITY

FEASTS AND FESTIVITY

How did this notion get round that women cook only for men? Why, indeed, should we manage with some cheese just because our sexual organs are different?

From *At Mrs Lipincote's*, 1945 | Elizabeth Taylor (1912–1975)

One cannot think well, love well, sleep well, if one has not dined well.

From *A Room of One's Own*, 1929 | Virginia Woolf (1882– 1941)

Life, itself, is the proper binge.

Julia Child (1912–2004)

Our three basic needs, for food and security and love are so mixed and mingled and entwined that we cannot straightly think of one without the others.

From *The Gastronomical Me*, 1943 | M F K Fisher (1908–1992)

A lot of people, cleverer and more learned than me, have written books about why people try to kill themselves. I prefer to think of the reasons I didn't.

An ambulance came, and took me to the hospital, and I sat in the waiting room of the duty psychiatrist, and suddenly, for the first time in a long time, I thought of baking: of a pie. I don't remember very much about the hospital itself (the brain is clever about forgetting things it would hurt you to remember), but I remember the pie, and I remember the way I worked through each ingredient, step by step, and how, when the duty psychiatrist asked me why, I could only think of shortcrust and soften the leeks in Irish butter until translucent and rub the butter into the flour and bind with milk. In the end I said, I don't know, which is so often the only way to try and explain suicide... They were talking, but I wasn't listening: instead I was thinking of pie.

And how I'd learned to make pastry with my grandmother, and how I wanted to cook again. It was like a little map: I will get through this, and I will cook something, and I will eat it, and I will be alive. I will be alive, and I will make something with my own two hands, and I will get through this. This too will pass – it has to – because there is a pie at the end. With a crisp crust and a soft yielding centre, and my first initial done in pastry at the top and brushed with golden egg, just like my grandmother used to do.

From *Midnight Chicken (& other recipes worth living for)*, 2019 |
Ella Risbridger (b.1992)

He began his soup – hers came at the same time, she had only toyed with some caviare by way of hors d'oeuvre, and it angered him to notice the obsequiousness of the waiters, who passed each thing to the dignified servant to be placed before the lady by his hand. Who was she to be served with such respect and rapidity...

Paul's irritation grew. 'She's well over thirty,' he said to himself. 'I suppose she has nothing else to live for! I wonder what the devil she'll eat next!'

She ate a delicate *truite bleue*, but she did not touch her wine again the while... What would her next course be? He found himself unpleasantly interested to know. The tenderest *selle d'agneau au lait* and the youngest green peas made their appearance, and again the maître d'hôtel returned, having mixed the salad.

Paul noticed with all these things the lady ate but a small portion of each. And it was not until a fat quail appeared later, while he himself was trying to get through two mutton chops *à l'anglaise*, that she again tasted her claret. Yes, it was claret, he felt sure, and probably wonderful claret at that. Confound her!...

What would she eat next? And why did it interest him what she ate or did not eat? The maître d'hôtel; again appeared with a dish of marvellous-looking nectarines. The waiter now handed the dignified servant the finger-bowl into which he poured rose-water. Paul could just distinguish the scent of it, and then he noticed the lady's hands. Yes, they at least were faultless, he could not cavil at them; slender and white, with that transparent whiteness like mother-of-pearl. And what pink nails! And how polished! Isabelle's hands – but he refused to think of them.

By this time he was conscious of an absorbing interest thrilling his whole being – disapproving irritated interest...

From *Three Weeks*, 1907 | Elinor Glyn (1864–1943)

'Godber's has come,' announced Sadie, issuing out of the pantry. She had seen the man pass the window.

That meant the cream puffs had come. Godber's were famous for their cream puffs. Nobody ever thought of making them at home.

'Bring them in and put them on the table, my girl,' ordered cook.

Sadie brought them in and went back to the door. Of course Laura and Jose were far too grown-up to really care about such things.

All the same, they couldn't help agreeing that the puffs looked very attractive. Very. Cook began arranging them, shaking off the extra icing sugar.

'Don't they carry one back to all one's parties?' said Laura.

'I suppose they do,' said practical Jose, who never liked to be carried back. 'They look beautifully light and feathery, I must say.'

'Have one each, my dears,' said cook in her comfortable voice. 'Yer ma won't know.'

Oh, impossible. Fancy cream puffs so soon after breakfast. The very idea made one shudder. All the same, two minutes later Laura and Jose were licking their fingers with that absorbed inward look that only comes from whipped cream

From *The Garden Party*, 1922 | Katherine Mansfield (1888–1923)

I am very glad the new Cook begins so well. Good apple pies are a considerable part of our domestic happiness.

Jane Austen (1775–1817) to Cassandra Austen, 17 October 1815

... an exquisite scent of olives and oil and juice rose from the great brown dish as Marthe, with a little flourish, took the cover off. The cook had spent three days over that dish. And she must take great care, Mrs Ramsay thought, diving into the soft mass, to choose a specially tender piece for William Bankes. And she peered into the dish, with its shiny walls and its confusion of savoury brown and yellow meats, and its bay leaves and its wine, and thought, This will celebrate the occasion - a curious sense rising in her, at once freakish and tender, of celebrating a festival...

'It is a triumph,' said Mr Bankes, laying his knife down for a moment. He had eaten attentively. It was rich; it was tender. It was perfectly cooked. How did she manage these things in the depths of the country? he asked her. She was a wonderful woman. All his love, all his reverence had returned, and she knew it.

From *To the Lighthouse*, 1927 | Virginia Woolf (1882–1941)

With her first bite of crayfish étouffée, Sidda could see her mother in the kitchen at Pecan Grove. She saw Vivi first melting butter in a large cast-iron skillet, then slowly stirring flour into the butter, and cooking the roux until it became a chestnut brown. She smelled the onions, celery, and green peppers as Vivi added them to the roux. She saw the dish change color as Vivi added the crayfish tails, along with fresh parsley, cayenne pepper, and generous shakes of the ever-present Tabasco bottle. With each bite, Sidda tasted her homeland and her mother's love.

After she paused to brush the tears from her eyes, Sidda said, 'So much good seasoning. It makes my eyes water'

'Right,' Teensy said.

'Tabasco and cayenne can do that,' Necie added.

From *Divine Secrets of the Ya-Ya Sisterhood*, 1996 | Rebecca Wells (b.1952)

My little love,

What am I to say to you, you naughty, extravagant, darling creature! The most exciting box brought by the postman struggling to the door at 7.30 this morning. It's a perfect morning and I woke up without a headache at all, feeling splendid. So I popped down and Mrs Calcraft made us both a cup of tea while I went 'up the garden' (where the daffodils are now blooming) and opened it right away. Asparagus, salted almonds, figs, dates. All the things I adore. Mrs Calcraft has never handled out-of-season asparagus before and is quite excited.

Winifred Holtby (1898–1935) to Vera Brittain, 2 April 1932

Eating was as close to heaven as my mother ever came. (In our day we have a name for a passion as disordered as hers.)

And almost as heavenly as eating was the making – how she gloried in it! Every last body on this earth has a particular notion of paradise, and this was hers, standing in the murderously hot back kitchen of her own house, concocting and contriving, leaning forward and squinting at the fine print of the cookery book, a clean wooden spoon in hand.

It is something to see, the way she concentrates, her hot, busy face, the way she thrills to see the dish take form as she pours the stewed fruit into the fancy mold, pressing the thickly cut bread down over the oozing juices, feeling it soften and absorb bit by bit a raspberry redness. Malvern pudding; she loves the words too, and feels them dissolve on her tongue like a sugary wafer, her tongue itself grown wafer-like and sweet. Like an artist – years later this form of artistry is perfectly clear to me – she stirs and arranges and draws in her brooding lower lip. Such a dish this will be. A warm sponge soaking up color...

Cuyler will be home from the quarry at five sharp; he will have himself a good cheerful wash at the kitchen basin, and by half-past five the two of them will sit down at the table – this very table, only spread with a clean cloth, every second day a clean cloth – and eat their supper. Which for the most part will be a silent meal, both my parents being shy by nature, and both brought up in the belief that conversing and eating are different functions, occupying separate trenches of time. Tonight they will partake of cold corned beef with a spoonful of homemade relish, some dressed potatoes at the side, cups of sweet tea, and then this fine pudding. His eyes will widen; my father, Cuyler Goodwill, aged, twenty-eight, two years married, will never in his life have tasted Malvern pudding. (That's what she's preparing for – his stunned and mild look of confusion, that tender, grateful male mouth dropping open in surprise. It's the least she can do, surprise him like this.) She sets a flower-patterned plate carefully on top of the pudding, and weights it with a stone.

From *The Stone Diaries*, 1993 | Carol Shields (1935–2003)

'I'm sorry we're late,' said Phoebe, looking around her suspiciously. This was not at all her kind of place, but she brightened up when the waitress approached their table with a tray of cakes, her tongs hovering.

Leonora from her corner looked annoyed, for she had been there longer and should have been served first. Still, she had her tea and that was a comfort.

'I'm going to have one of those marron things,' said Jennifer. 'Oh, but there seems to be only one – would you like it, Phoebe?'

'No, you have it. I'd rather have a strawberry tart.'

The waitress went over to Leonora's table. 'I'm sorry, madam, she said in answer to her request, 'that young lady over there had the last marron gâteau.'

'Oh, but this is really too annoying, said Leonora petulantly. 'I've just been to the dentist – I can't eat anything hard.'

'None of the gâteaux is hard, madam,' said the waitress reproachfully. 'They're all fresh today.'

'Well, then, a coffee éclair.' Leonora glared – and even a person as lovely and gracious as Leonora could do this when the occasion demanded it – in the direction of the table where Phoebe and Jennifer and her mother were sitting. But the undistinguished-looking women, the older one inelegantly surrounded by shopping, the younger ones dressed most unsuitably for town and carrying flower-patterned paper carrier bags, seemed hardly worthy of her attention and she soon forgot them in the pleasure of the eclair, which was almost as delicious as the marron confection would have been.

Only a retired Brazilian diplomat, the type of man who could spare the time for afternoon tea, sitting at a table midway between the protagonists, noticed the little drama, if such it was. Now what have I seen? he asked himself? Something or nothing? A beautiful woman disappointed over a cake, a mere triviality, really, and yet who could tell..?

From *The Sweet Dove Died*, 1978 | Barbara Pym (1913–1980)

The preparation of food, getting meals, is work more positive in nature and often more agreeable than cleaning. First of all it means marketing, often the bright spot of the day .... The housewife knows little of winning in games, but a solid cabbage, a ripe Camembert, are treasures that must be cleverly won from the unwilling storekeeper; the game is to get the best for the least money; economy means not so much helping with the budget as winning the game. She is pleased with her passing triumph as she contemplates her well-filled larder.

Gas and electricity have killed the magic of fire, but in the country many women still know the joy of kindling live flames from inert wood. With her fire going, woman becomes a sorceress; by a simple movement, as in beating eggs, or through the magic of fire, she effects the transmutation of substances: matter becomes food. There is enchantment in these alchemies, there is poetry in making preserves; the housewife has caught duration in the snare of sugar, she has enclosed life in jars. Cooking is revelation and creation; and a woman can find special satisfaction in a successful cake or a flaky pastry, for not everyone can do it: one must have the gift.

From *The Second Sex*, translated by H M Parshley, 1940 |
Simone de Beauvoir (1908–1986)

Quilting bees were eagerly anticipated by southern black women. They offered the only nonlabor, nonreligious occasions where women could gather and exchange all the communities' good and bad news. The women planned for weeks. Then they selected and cooked their favorite dessert dishes and brought them to the gathering. The bees were always held in the back of the store, which meant that Bailey and I could look forward to some delicious cakes and pies and, if the event took place in the summer, some luscious hand-cranked strawberry ice cream. Usually cranked by us.

Mrs. Sneed, the pastor's wife, would bring sweet potato pie, warm and a little too sweet for Momma's taste but perfect to Bailey and me. Mrs Miller's coconut cake and Mrs Kendrick's chocolate fudge were what Adam and Eve ate in the Garden just before the Fall. But the most divine dessert of all was Momma's Caramel Cake.

Momma would labor prayerfully over her selection, because she knew but would never admit that she and all the women were in hot competition over whose culinary masterpiece was the finest.

Momma could bake all the other women's dishes and often made them for the family, but not one of the other cooks would even dare the Caramel Cake (always to be spoken of in capital letters). Since she didn't have brown sugar, she had to make her own caramel syrup. Making her caramel cake took four to five hours, but the result was worthy of the labor. The salty sweetness of the caramel frosting along with the richness of the batter made the dessert soften and liquefy on the tongue and slip quietly down the throat almost without notice. Save that it left a memory of heaven itself in the mouth.

From *Hallelujah! The Welcome Table*, 2007 | Maya Angelou (1928–2014)

When I was eleven we all moved to the country. We had a cow, and chickens, and partly because of that and partly because grandmother had died we began to eat more richly.

We had chocolate puddings with chopped nuts and heavy cream. The thought of them makes me dizzy now, but we loved them. And lots of butter: I was good at churning, and learned very well how to sterilize the wooden churn and make the butter and then roll it into fine balls and press it into molds. I liked that. And we could have mayonnaise, rich yellow with eggs and oil, instead of the boiled dressing Grandmother's despotic bowels and stern palate called for.

Mother, in an orgy of baking brought on probably by all the beautiful eggs and butter lying around, spent every Saturday morning making cakes. They were piled high with icings. They were filled with crushed almonds, chopped currants, and an outrageous number of calories. They were beautiful. Saturday afternoon they sat cooling, along with Mother and the kitchen after the hectic morning, and by Saturday night they were already a pleasant if somewhat bilious memory.

...I learned a lot about cakes from her. The fact that I have never made one since then – at least, the kind with many layers and fillings and icings and all that – has little to do with the gratitude I have often felt for knowing how to measure and sift and be patient and not be daunted by disappointment...

...The stove, the bins, the cupboards, I had learned forever, make an inviolable throne room. From them I ruled; temporarily I controlled. I felt powerful and I loved that feeling.

I am more modest now, but I still think that one of the pleasantest of all emotions is to know that I, I with my brains and my hands, have nourished my beloved few, that I have concocted a stew or a story, a rarity or a plain dish, to sustain them truly against the hungers of the world.

From *The Gastronomical Me*, 1943 | M F K Fisher (1908–1992)

When I was six, my mother consulted her GP, complaining that my diet consisted almost exclusively of chocolate-coated digestive biscuits and glasses of milk. He observed sensibly that I would grow out of it, although I doubt whether he realised how long it would take...

By the time I arrived at university my attitude to the food I had heard about but never tasted – French, Indian, Chinese, Italian – was very much like my idea of sex. I longed to try them both but needed time to overcome years of hostile propaganda (if there was one thing my mother disapproved of more than foreign food, it was sex.) In the end I shook off both sets of inhibitions together, losing my virginity and going to an Indian restaurant for the first time in the same month, I'm not sure in which order...

Then, in the Eighties, I fell hopelessly and permanently in love. Having discovered my consuming passion, Italian food, I abandoned fruitless searches for obscure Thai ingredients in favour of simpler pleasures: grilled porcini slithering voluptuously on the tongue, the crunch of courgette flowers fried in batter, prosciutto slices crumpled on a plate with over-ripe figs...

From *Hungry For You*, 1996 | Joan Smith (b.1953)

The supper was delicious. There was home-made crusty bread, hot onion soup, delicious rabbit stew, baked apples in a silver dish, honey, butter the colour of marigolds, a big blue jug of warm mulled claret, and hot roasted chestnuts folded in a napkin.

Miss Heliotrope confined herself to eating bread and butter and sipping a little claret, but she did it with an appetite that surprised her. Maria ate everything there was to eat, very daintily, as was her habit, but with an enjoyment surprising in one so ethereal-looking. Her cousin greeted her good appetite with a chuckle of appreciation. 'A digestion of cast iron, like all the Merryweathers,' he noted with approval. 'Your little dog, also, I note, is a good trencherman.'

From *The Little White Horse*, 1946 | Elizabeth Goudge (1900–1984)

They dried each other off. Mira put on a heavy terry robe, and Ben wrapped a towel around himself.

'I'm hungry,' she said.

'I'm famished,' he said.

Together, they pulled everything out of the refrigerator, and produced a feast of Jewish salami and feta cheese and hard-boiled eggs and tomatoes and black bread and sweet butter and half-sour pickles and big black Greek olives and raw Spanish onions and beer, and trotted all of it back to bed with them and sat there gorging themselves and talking and drinking and laughing and touching each other with tender fingertips. And finally they set the platters and plates and beer cans on the floor ...

From *The Women's Room*, 1977 | Marilyn French (1929–2009)

My mother was barely five foot one, but I felt like she was six foot two. She was smart and tough and fierce and protective. She was generous, loyal and funny. She had only two goals in life: to raise her two daughters and to end breast cancer. She pushed us hard and with high expectations as she nurtured us. And all the while, she made Maya and me feel special, like we could do anything.

When I would come home from the Sheltons', I'd usually find my mother reading or working on her notes or preparing to make us dinner. Breakfast aside [my mother] loved to cook, and I loved to sit with her in the kitchen and watch and smell and eat. She had a giant

Chinese-style cleaver that she chopped with, and a cupboard full of spices. I loved that okra could be soul food or Indian food, depending on what spices you chose; she would add dried shrimp and sausage to make it like gumbo, or fry it up with turmeric and mustard seeds.

My mother cooked like a scientist. She was always experimenting – an oyster beef stir-fry one night, potato latkes on another. Even my lunch became a lab for her creations: On the bus, my friends, with their bologna sandwiches and PB&Js, would ask excitedly, 'Kamala, what you got?' I'd open the brown paper bag, which my mother always decorated with a smiley face or a doodle: 'Cream cheese and olives on dark rye!' I'll admit, not every experiment was successful – at least not for my grade school palate. But no matter what, it was different, and that made it special, just like my mother.

From *The Truths We Hold: An American Journey*, 2019 | Kamala Harris (b.1964)

On this stormy day the film star Romy Schneider had died. Grandma was in tears. In honour of Romy, a bit more money than usual had been spent, there was oeufs mayo and leeks vinaigrette, a hunk of beef, pot-roasted with tomatoes and carrots and cut into soft slices, salad and Roquefort. The bathroom in that apartment was housed in a few sheets of corrugated iron and had a rickety door; it was a demarcation rather than a room. The family was not well off, and yet food was always prepared with care. Grandma continued to sob, looking through her Romy Schneider cuttings, and we quietly ate baked pears.

From *How To Eat a Peach*, 2018 | Diana Henry (b.1963)

I've been learning Mandarin for over three years now but there are still days when language fails me, when food feels like the only thing I have to tie me to this other home my family brought to me from far away.

There are things that pass from one hand to another, from mothers to daughters, from sister to sister, between cousins, between friends. A hot curry puff fresh from the oven, a secret batter recipe, a special technique for slicing mango.

One day I tried making [my grandmother's] curry in my flat in Wellington. I read all the ingredients labels of all the curry powders in the supermarket to find the closest match: coriander seeds, cumin, fennel, chilli, turmeric, cinnamon, cloves, pepper, cardamom. The richly-scented list repeated like an incantation in my head. I bought fresh roti canai from Kelburn Parade and carried it home through a southerly storm. The curry turned out badly: watery, flavourless, the aubergine overcooked. But for a while my little kitchen smelled like cumin and coconut and crushed ginger. Like running in from the tropical rain, like Popo ladling rice into our bowls, like the lit mosquito coil and the flame lighting up my mother's hands as she carries it towards me. These things I don't need language to understand.

From *Tiny Moons: A Year of Eating in Shanghai*, 2020 | Nina Mingya Powles (b.1993)

I wonder if the ladies of Overton used some of the innocent flowers, the aconite, the primroses, the polyanthus, grown by Samuel Cooke the gardener to decorate the creams and trifles and custards which surely figured among their desserts at the festive season. How ravishing those eighteenth-century tables must have looked when the crystallised fruit, the oranges and raisins, the spun sugar confections, the trays of syllabubs, the pyramids of jellies, the dishes of little almond cakes shaped into knots and rings and bows, the marchpanes spiked with candied fruits, the curd tarts and all the sweetmeats were spread. No doubts many such delicacies were made in their own stillrooms by the ladies of the household.

From *Is There a Nutmeg in the House?*, 2000 | Elizabeth David (1913–1992)

The place I like best in this world is the kitchen. No matter where it is, no matter what kind, if it's a kitchen, if it's a place where they make food, it's fine by me. Ideally it should be well broken in. Lots of tea towels, dry and immaculate. White tile catching the light (ting! ting!).

I love even incredibly dirty kitchens to distraction – vegetable droppings all over the floor, so dirty your slippers turn black on the bottom. Strangely, it's better if this kind of kitchen is large. I lean up against the silver door of a towering, giant refrigerator stocked with enough food to get through a winter. When I raise my eyes from the oil-spattered gas burner and the rusty kitchen knife, outside the window stars are glittering, lonely.

Now only the kitchen and I are left. It's just a little nicer than being all alone.

When I'm dead worn out, in a reverie, I often think that when it comes time to die, I want to breathe my last in a kitchen. Whether it's cold and I'm all alone, or somebody's there and it's warm, I'll stare death fearlessly in the eye. If it's a kitchen, I'll think, 'How good.'

From *Kitchen*, 1993 | Banana Yoshimoto (b.1964)

Oh, what a joy to get a real calf's foot from the butcher, she thought, and not to have to cheat by putting in gelatine. The small things of life were often so much bigger than the great things, she decided, wondering how many writers and philosophers had said this before her, the trivial pleasures like cooking, one's home, little poems especially sad ones, solitary walks, funny things seen and overheard.

From *Less Than Angels*, 1955 | Barbara Pym (1913–1980)

I was hungry but I didn't feel like cooking, so I had the most beautiful lunch of cold baked beans – what bliss it is that we can now afford things in tins again! I had bread-and-butter, too, and lettuce and cold rice pudding and two slices of cake (real shop cake) and milk. Hel and Ab [the animals] sat on the table and were given treats – they had had their own dinners, of course. They both took to baked beans at once – there is precious little they don't take to. Heloise even accepted salted lettuce. (During our famine period she became practically a vegetarian.) Then, all three of us very full, we had a sleep in the four-poster, Ab curled up at the foot and Hel with her back against my chest, which was rather hot but always gives one a companionable feeling.

From *I Capture the Castle*, 1948 | Dodie Smith (1896–1990)

From *Goblin Market*

"Our grapes fresh from the vine,
Pomegranates full and fine,
Dates and sharp bullaces,
Rare pears and greengages,
Damsons and blueberries,
Taste them and try:
Currants and gooseberries,

Bright-fire-like barberries,
Figs to fill your mouth,
Citrus from the South
Sweet to tongue and sound to eye;
Come buy, come buy."

Christine Rossetti (1830–1894)

It's been so arduous, Edi's dying. It's like we've all been digging and digging, shoveling out a hole, and we can finally stop. Only there's this hole here.

Which is no reason not to make French toast! Or so seems to be the thinking of Honey and Belle, who are in the kitchen, frying up platters full of it, custardy and buttery and perfect, plates and forks and maple syrup passed around the living room. Honey has also cut a couple of pink grapefruits into skinny half-moons, and it's just what I didn't know I needed: bracing and delicious. Cedar has his guitar out, and he and Jules are singing quietly together with Jonah, 'Hey Jude', and all the other Edi favorites. Okay, okay, I think, to nobody in particular. Consider life affirmed. It's also possible that I'm drunk.

From *We All Want Impossible Things*, 2022 | Catherine Newman (b.1968)

The first memories of their idyll abounded only in images of perfect food, choice fruits, and the pleasures of a country larder. She would see an exhausted Chéri - paler in the blazing sunlight - dragging himself through the tunnels of trees in Normandy, or asleep on the warm paving stones by a pond. Léa would wake Chéri to stuff him with strawberries, with cream, with frothy milk, and corn-fed chicken. As if dazed, with wide blank eyes, he would sit at dinner watching the flight of the moths round the bowl of roses, and look at his watch to see if it was time to go to bed: while Léa, disappointed but unresentful, reflected on the unfulfilled promises of the kiss at Neuilly and good-naturedly bided her time.

From *Chéri*, 1920 | Colette (1873–1954)

I don't deny that food, its preparation as much as its consumption, is about sharing, about connectedness. But that's not all that it's about. There seems to me to be something robustly affirmative about taking trouble to feed yourself; enjoying life on purpose, rather than by default...

The solitary diner can sometimes, if not often, eat lobster alone. I buy it cooked and cold and I fry some bacon to eat with it. I might make mayonnaise. I don't mind what I have to do to it or how I eat my lobster: salad, club sandwich (toast some brioche, just see). The pleasure lies in the solitary indulgence.

My most intense solitary indulgence, without question, is grouse; 12 August figures strongly in my diary. I'm not the type to go wading across moors, but I don't mind paying for my pleasures...

From *How to Eat*, 1998 | Nigella Lawson (b.1960)

Widgeon, Roast

Ingredients. – Widgeons, a little flour, butter. Mode. – These are trussed in the same manner as wild duck, but must not be kept so long before they are dressed. Put them down to a brisk fire; flour, and baste them continuously with butter, and, when browned and nicely frothed, send them to the table hot and quickly. Serve with brown gravy, or orange gravy, and a cut lemon. Time. – ¼ hour; if liked well done, 20 minutes. Average cost, Is. each but seldom bought. Sufficient. – 2 for a dish. Seasonable from October to February.

From *Mrs Beeton's Dictionary of Every-Day Cookery*, 1865 | Mrs Beeton (1836–1865)

Water Souchy
Perch, tench, soles, eels, and flounders are considered the best fish for this dish. For the souchy, put some water into a stewpan with a bunch of chopped parsley, some roots, and sufficient salt to make it brackish. Let these simmer for I hour, and then stew the fish in this water. When they are done, take them out to drain, have ready some finely-chopped parsley, and a few roots cut into slices of about one inch thick and an inch in length. Pat the fish into a tureen or deep dish, strain the liquor over them, and add the minced parsley and roots. Serve with brown bread and butter.

From *Mrs Beeton's Dictionary of Every-Day Cookery*, 1865 | Mrs Beeton (1836–1865)

Her hand has lost its cunning - the firm, true hand that wrote these formulae, and penned the information contained in this little book. Cold in the silent tomb lie the once useful, nimble fingers, - now nerveless, unable for anything, and ne'er to do work more in this world! Exquisite palate, unerring judgement, sound common sense, refined tastes, - all these had the dear Lady who has gone ere her youth had scarcely come. But four times seven years were all she passed in this world; and since the day she became wedded wife - now nearly nine years past - her greatest, chiefest aims were to provide for the comfort and pleasure of those she loved and hard around her, and to employ her best faculties for the use of her sisters, Englishwomen generally...

Samuel Orchart Beeton in *Mrs Beeton's Dictionary of Every-Day Cookery*, 1865 | Mrs Beeton (1836–1865)

Wednesday, 26 November, 1941

My bony mutton made a lovely casserole. I first fried it and then added onion, celery, carrot and turnip; I cooked it very slowly all morning by the dining-room fire, and added potatoes to it three-quarters of an hour before lunch. On the other side of the fire, I had my big pan with the suet pudding in, and it was really one of the best puddings I've made for a long time. I minced the suet from the kidney I had bought with the meat, and also two slices of wholemeal bread and two strips of my candied peel, made by boiling orange peel till tender with a little honey and water... The sauce was a problem – NO milk for it, not even a tiny drop, with so little being allowed. Finally, I made custard sauce with water, and added honey as a sweetener. I am trying to save my extra sugar to make marmalade after Christmas. At lunch-time my husband said, 'This is the nicest casserole we have had for a long time.' It had done so perfectly that there was no liquid – just tender, juicy vegetables and meat. When I served the pudding, I said carelessly, 'Oh, I've made clear honey sauce for a change.' I know that one, he doesn't like economy dishes – if he realises they are economy dishes! He said, 'By Gad, it's grand – and brings out the real favour of the pudding.' Gladys and I laughed afterwards, but she said, 'If I'd not seen you make that pudding, I would never have believed it.'

Diary entry, 26 November 1941, from *Nella Last's War*, 1981 | Nella Last (1889–1968)

Harriet was not going to be cheated of her Sunday roast...

From *Some Tame Gazelle*, 1950 | Barbara Pym (1913–1980)

Thursday 10 September [1822, Calais]
Dined on gravy soup, stewed eel, a hot *fricandeau de veau* & a little hashed hare, both very good. Fritters, dropt thro' a spoon with a round hole an inch in diameter at the bottom of it, light & excellent. Swiss cheese Gruyère (3 francs a lb) & pears. A bottle of common wine of which I had only about 3 glasses...

From *I Know My Own Heart: The Diaries of Anne Lister* | Anne Lister (1791–1840)

So Sofie and I have come to Pizzeria da Michele, and these pies we have just ordered - one for each of us - are making us lose our minds. I love my pizza so much, in fact, that I have come to believe in my delirium, that my pizza might actually love me, in return. I am having a relationship with this pizza, almost an affair... How was I to have known there could be a crust in this world that was thin and doughy? Holy of holies! Thin, doughy, strong, gummy, yummy, chewy, salty pizza paradise. On top, there is a sweet tomato sauce that foams up all bubbly and creamy when it melts the fresh buffalo mozzarella, and the one sprig of basil in the middle of the whole deal somehow infuses the entire pizza with herbal radiance, much the same way one shimmering movie star in the middle of a party brings a contact high of glamour to everyone around her. It's technically impossible to eat this thing, of course. You try to take a bite off your slice and the gummy crust folds, and the hot cheese runs away like topsoil in a landslide, makes a mess of you and your surroundings, but just deal with it.

From *Eat, Pray, Love*, 2006 | Elizabeth Gilbert (b.1969)

She snoops about the larder
For sundry small supplies,
She breaks the little crusty bits
Off rims of apple pies,
She pokes the roast-potato-dish
When Sunday dinner's done,
And if there are two left in it
Griselda snitches one;
Cold chicken and cold cauliflower
She pulls in little chunks –
And when Cook calls:
'What are you doing there?'
Griselda bunks.

Griselda is greedy. Well, that's how she feels,
She simply can't help eating in-between meals
And always forgets what it's leading to, though
The Doctor has frequently told her: 'You know
Why, don't you?'
When the stomach-ache starts and Griselda says: 'Oh!'

She slips down to the dining room
When everyone's in bed,
For cheese-rind on the supper-tray,
For buttered crusts of bread,
A biscuit from the biscuit-box,
Lump sugar from the bowl,
A gherkin from the pickle-jar,
Are all Griselda's toll:
She tastes the salted almonds,
And she tries the candied fruits –

And when Dad shouts:
'Who is it down below?'
Griselda scoots.

Griselda is greedy. Her relatives scold,
And tell her how sorry she'll be when she's old,
She will lose her complexion, she's sure to grow fat,
She will spoil her inside - does she know what she's at? -
(Why do they?)
Some people are greedy. Leave it at that.

Eleanor Farjeon (1881–1965)

I drink sherry and wine by myself because I like it and I get the sensuous feeling of indulgence I do when I eat salted nuts or cheese; luxury, bliss, erotic-tinged.

Diary entry, 25 February 1956 | Sylvia Plath (1932–1963)

If I had my way - and I shan't - my Christmas Day eating and drinking would consist of an omelette and cold ham and a nice bottle of wine at lunch time, and a smoked salmon sandwich with a glass of champagne on a tray in bed in the evening. This lovely selfish anti-gorging, un-Christmas dream of hospitality, either given or taken, must be shared by thousands of women who know it's all Lombard Street to a China orange that they'll spend both Christmas Eve and Christmas morning peeling, chopping, mixing, boiling roasting, steaming. That they will eat and drink too much, that someone will say the turkey isn't quite as good as last year, or discover that the rum for the pudding has been forgotten.

From *Is There a Nutmeg in the House?*, 2000 | Elizabeth David (1913–1992)

Oh an English Christmas! We are not Christians; we are not social; we have no part in the fabric of the world, but, all the same, Christmas flattens us out like a steam roller; turkey, pudding, tips, waits, holly, good wishes, presents, sweets; so here we sit, on Boxing day, at Rodmell, over a wood fire, & I can only rouse myself by thinking of you.

Virginia Woolf (1882–1941) to Jacques Raverat, 26 December 1924

Each week one of us would host a party to raise money and to raise our spirits. The hostess had to serve special dyansyin foods to bring good fortune of all kinds – dumplings shaped like silver money ingots, long rice noodles for long life, boiled peanuts for conceiving sons, and of course, many good-luck oranges for a plentiful, sweet life.

'What fine food we treated ourselves to with our meager allowances! We didn't notice that the dumplings were stuffed mostly with stringy squash and that the oranges were spotted with wormy holes. We ate sparingly, not as if we didn't have enough, but to protest how we could not eat another bite, we had already bloated ourselves from earlier in the day. We knew we had luxuries few people could afford. We were the lucky ones.'

From *The Joy Luck Club*, 1989 | Amy Tan (b.1952)

The tea was really amazing – tomato sandwiches, with the crusts cut off, little hot French pancakes, bread and butter, slices of sweet tea buns buttered, apricot jam and little homemade pastries and cakes .... The china and silverware were like the tablecloths, pre-war in their condition. Everything was exquisitely kept and served, a treat if it had only been bread and butter and the really good hot tea, with unlimited milk and sugar – and the tea was 2s a head! I felt I wanted to linger and then walk round the well-kept grounds, down to the water's edge, where the lawn sloped to the quiet backwater end of the lake. I enjoyed the food I'd not see before it was set before me, but even more the luxury and comfort. Not one little hint or sign of utility or make do and mend. I felt I'd have liked a holiday there but realise it would pall on my husband...

Diary entry, 26 October 1947, from *Nella Last's Peace*, 2008 | Nella Last (1889–1968)

Flora had arranged two kinds of food for the two kinds of guests she was expecting. For the Starkadders and such of the local thorny peasantry as would attend there were syllabubs, ice-pudding, caviare sandwiches, crab patties, trifle and champagne. For the County was cider, cold home-cured ham, home-made bread and salads made from local fruit. The table from which the County were to feed was rich with cottage flowers. The rosy efflorescence of the peonies floated above the table from which the peasantry would eat.

Wreaths of little flowers, like chains of little gems, hung from the rafters. Their reds, oranges, blues, and pinks glowed against the soft, sooty-black of the ceiling and walls. The air smelled sweet of cherry-pie and fruit salad. Outside the sun flamed in glory; and inside the kitchen there were these sweet smells and cool, delicious-looking food.

Flora took a last look round, and was utterly satisfied.

From *Cold Comfort Farm*, 1932 | Stella Gibbons (1902–1989)

The other peak experience came after a splendid walk to Dog Cove – a walk through great trees, moss underfoot and the leaves of many wildflowers to note, mushrooms, great lichen-covered rocks looming up, and the broken light through birch and ash leaves... we spread a blanket and had our picnic, fish chowder and a great salad of hard-boiled eggs, lettuce and blue cheese with French dressing, and a Bartlett pear.

And then the silence fell.

Diary entry, 26 September, from *Recovering: A Journal 1978–1979* | May Sarton (1912–1995)

I believe in parties. If you have parties to mark the fact that people have died, I think you should certainly make an effort to mark the fact that you were born and are still alive.

I didn't think I would face my fiftieth birthday without a partner, a family, a regular income or a job. But there you are. It's no reason not to have a party.

From *The Art of Not Falling Apart*, 2019 | Christina Patterson (b.1963)

While our two young men were away Katherine [Mansfield] and I sat at the fire darning our husbands' socks and talking of our homes and childhoods. We conjured up the excitement of the day of a party: the preparations, washing our hair and plaiting it to make it wavy, putting 'baby' ribbons in our camisoles; the wonderful feeling of pleasurable anticipation while waiting till the last moment to put on the party dress; then the hooking-up, the few stitches, and the running from room to room to look in the glass; the nice faint smell of the long white kid gloves, the white silk stockings and satin slippers.

I think she found it easy to be with me; we had something in common when we first met, a memory of childhood in a distant provincial setting in another land. It was rather as if we were both exiles and did not quite 'belong' in London, but we both loved being alive in this wonderful, beautiful, tortuous, and often torturing world.

From *Today We Will Only Gossip*, 1964 | Beatrice, Lady Glenavy (1863–1970)

Before I was born my mother was in great agony of spirit and in a tragic situation. She could take no food except iced oysters and champagne. If people ask me when I began to dance I reply, 'In my mother's womb, probably as a result of the oysters and champagne–the food of Aphrodite'.

From *My Life*, 1927 | Isadora Duncan (1827–1927)

The dear girl was married on the 23rd, the same day as Mother's wedding. A lovely day, the house full of sunshine, flowers, friends, and happiness. Uncle S J May married them, with no fuss, but much love, and we all stood round her. She in her silver-gray silk, with lilies of the valley (John's flower) in her bosom and hair. We in gray thin stuff and roses, - sackcloth, I called it, and ashes of roses, for I mourn the loss of my Nan, and am not comforted. We have had a little feast, sent by good Mrs Judge Shaw, then the old folks danced round the bridal pair on the lawn in the German fashion, making a pretty picture to remember, under our Revolutionary elm.

Then, with tears and kisses, our dear girl, in her little white bonnet, went happily away with her good John, and we ended our first wedding. Mr Emerson [*Ralph Waldo Emerson*] kissed her, and I thought that honor would make even matrimony endurable, for he is the god of my idolatry, and has been for years.

Diary entry, May 1860, *on the wedding of her sister Anna* ('Meg' in *Little Women*) | Louisa May Alcott (1832–1888)

The prospect of the Netherfield ball was extremely agreeable to every female of the family. Mrs Bennet chose to consider it as given in compliment to her eldest daughter, and was particularly flattered by receiving the invitation from Mr. Bingley himself, instead of a ceremonious card. Jane pictured to herself a happy evening in the society of her two friends, and the attentions of their brother; and Elizabeth thought with pleasure of dancing a great deal with Mr. Wickham, and of seeing a confirmation of everything in Mr. Darcy's look and behaviour. The happiness anticipated by Catherine and Lydia depended less on any single event, or any particular person, for though they each, like Elizabeth, meant to dance half the evening with Mr. Wickham, he was by no means the only partner who could satisfy them, and a ball was, at any rate, a ball. And even Mary could assure her family that she had no disinclination for it.

From *Pride and Prejudice*, 1813 | Jane Austen (1775–1817)

General de Burgh is to give a ball for the new year day. These words make my heart beat as if it would jump out of my breast. Beat for anxiety, wish, fear. I wish to go, I fear to be asked, and if I am asked to stay at home, then I hope, then I fear again, and can think of nothing else. God forgive me if it be a sin.

Diary entry, 1796 | Eugenia Wynne (1780–1853)

The ball, the ball always trots in my head. I cannot help but I am always thinking of it.

Diary entry, the following day, 1796 | Eugenia Wynne (1780–1853)

We could see that people had started to dance inside the house.

The man who cried at the funeral pushed me towards the door. 'Come on, your dress is so lovely, let's dance, let's dance, let's dance.'

We danced as if it was our very last night on earth – and to celebrate his new love and my new freedom and to celebrate my having been nominated for a big literary prize and to a thousand and one nights without pain, and because, as he puts it, 'life is as fragile as glass slipper'. I didn't quite get that, but he said he'd had too much champagne so maybe he meant a glass coffin – which was even more bewildering, but then he was The Man Who Cried at the Funeral.

We kicked off our shoes just like the song that was being played told us to do. Three luscious red velvet sofas had been pushed against the walls. We whirled and leapt around and sweated and then a striped kitten slunk onto the dance floor, like a tiny leopard, its tail raised. I gently lifted it up from the feet of the crowd and placed it on top of my new friend's head.

'I can feel it purring through my fingers,' he said. At that moment I thought the tempest was over. I was ready to do something I had never done before – like write a manifesto in the toilet wall in a pub.

I believe in people who are nervous and whose hands shake a little.

From *The Cost of Living*, 2018 | Deborah Levy (b.1959)

Well, it has been three days since my debut party started but I finally got tired and left the party last night and went to bed because I always seem to lose all of my interest in a party after a few days, but Dorothy never loses her interest in a party and when I woke up this morning Dorothy was just saying goodbye to some of the guests. I mean Dorothy seems to have quite a lot of vitality, because the last guests at the party were guest we picked up when the party went to take a swim at Long Beach the day before yesterday and they were practically fresh, but Dorothy had gone clear through the party from beginning to end without even stopping to go to a Turkish bath as most of the gentlemen had to do.

From *Gentlemen Prefer Blondes*, 1925 | Anita Loos (1889–1981)

Midsummer Day and, yes, it's her birthday again - she who scribes this page. There was a bumper post from most of the right people, and the rest, I know, are too busy. So I enjoyed all the letters that came and spent the afternoon answering some of them. Jack and I went out in the car to the butcher and the village, where I stood in a queue for peas, potatoes, asparagus and tomatoes, for this evening we had a birthday meal. And didn't we enjoy it, complete with half of the half-bottle of Graves?

Diary entry, 14 June 1944, from *Mrs Milburn's diaries: an Englishwoman's day-to-day reflections, 1939–1945* | Clara Milburn (1883–1961)

I must go to the dogs again some time, Sarah promised herself. She had the gift of being pleased by any form of pleasure. It never surprised her when her Sixth Form girls deserted their homework for dancing, speed tracks or the films. She sympathised with them.

The road curved near the estuary again. A group of huts and railway carriages were hung with strings of red and gold and green electric lights like garlands. The bus halted beside it. Sarah could read a notice 'Amicable Jack Brown's Open Air Cafe. Known in every Port in the World. Open all Night.'

She was enchanted. Oh, I must come here. I'll bring the staff. It'll do us all good.

She saw herself drinking beer with a domestic science teacher among the sailors at two o'clock in the morning. The proper technique of headmistress-ship was to break all the rules of decorum and justify the breach.

'Oh, lovely world,' thought Sarah, in love with life and all its varied richness.

From *South Riding*, 1936 | Winifred Holtby (1898–1935)

From *Weekend Glory*

My job at the plant
ain't the biggest bet,
but I pay my bills
and stay out of debt.
I get my hair done for my own self's sake,
so I don't have to pick
and I don't have to rake.

Take the church money out
and head cross town
to my friend girl's house
where we plan our round.
We meet our men and go to a joint
where the music is blue
and to the point.

Folks write about me.
They just can't see
how I work all week
at the factory.

Then get spruced up
and laugh and dance
And turn away from worry
with sassy glance.

They accuse me of livin'
from day to day.
but who are they kiddin'?
So are they.

My life ain't heaven
but it sure ain't hell
I'm not on top
but I call it swell
If I'm able to work
and get paid right
and have the luck to be Black
on a Saturday.

Maya Angelou (1928–2014)

'I'm going to tell Aunt Izzie that I don't like you,' declared Dorry, putting one leg through the opening in the door.

'No you aren't,' said Katy, seizing him, 'you are going to stay, because now we are going to have the feast! Do stop, Phil; and Johnnie, don't be a goose, but come and pass round the cookies.'

The word 'feast' produced a speedy effect on the spirits of the party. Phil cheered at once, and Dorry changed his mind about going. The black bottle was solemnly set in the midst, and the cookies were handed about by Johnnie, who was now all smiles. The cookies had scalloped edges and caraway seeds inside, and were very nice. There were two apiece, and as the last was finished, Katy put her hand in her pocket, and, amid great applause, produced the crowning addition to the repast – seven long brown sticks of cinnamon.

'Isn't it fun?' she said. 'Debbie was real good-natured to-day, and let me put my own hand into the box, so I picked out the longest sticks there were. Now, Cecy, as you're company, you shall have the first drink out of the bottle.'

The 'something delicious' proved to be weak vinegar-and-water. It was quite warm, but somehow, drunk up there in the loft, and out of a bottle, it tasted very nice. Besides, they didn't call it vinegar-and-water – of course not! Each child gave his or her swallow a different name, as if the bottle were like Signor Blitz's and could pour out a dozen things at once. Clover called her share 'Raspberry Shrub,' Dorry christened his 'Ginger Pop,' while Cecy, who was romantic, took here three sips under the name of 'Hydomel,' which she explained was something nice, made, she believed, of beeswax.

From *What Katy Did*, 1872 | 'Susan M Coolidge' (1835–1905)

Went to Gloucester for a fortnight with May at the Mansfield's [sic]. Found a family of six pretty daughters, a pleasant mother, & a father who was the image of one of the Cheeryble Brothers. Had a jolly time boating, driving, charading dancing & picnicing. One mild moonlight night a party of us camped out on Norman's Woe & had a splendid time, lying on the rocks singing, talking, sleeping & rioting up & down. We had a fine time & took coffee at all hours. The moon rose & set beautifully, & the sunrise was a picture I shall never forget.

Diary entry, August 1864 | Louisa May Alcott (1832–1888)

Imagine, if you can, what the rest of the evening was like. How they crouched by the fire which blazed and leaped and made much of itself in the little grate. How they removed the covers of the dishes, and found rich, hot, savory soup, which was a meal in itself, and sandwiches and toast and muffins enough for both of them. The mug from the washstand was used as Becky's tea cup, and the tea was so delicious that it was not necessary to pretend that it was anything but tea. They were warm and full-fed and happy, and it was just like Sara that, having found her strange good fortune real, she should give herself up to the enjoyment of it to the utmost. She had lived such a life of imaginings that she was quite equal to accepting any wonderful thing that happened, and almost to cease, in a short time, to find it bewildering.

'I don't know anyone in the world who could have done it,' she said, 'but there has been someone. And here we are sitting by their fire – and – and – it's true! And whoever it is – whoever they are – I have a friend, Becky – someone is my friend.'

From *A Little Princess*, 1905 | Frances Hodgson Burnett (1849–1924)

Their happiness was then complete. Their husbands would not have known them.

From *The Enchanted April*, 1922 | Elizabeth von Arnim (1866–1941)

The other day, while digging through a box of documents, I found a bit of my mother's writing. It was a recipe she had jotted down after someone suggested she write a sequel to my novel *The Kitchen God's Wife*, which she felt was close to her true story. She would call her book *The Kitchen God's Wife Cookbook*. She was indeed an excellent cook, but she was not able to organize her knowledge into precise amounts of ingredients and clear instructions. Her method of explanation ran more toward a haphazard list of ingredients without quantities. She was an intuitive cook. 'The recipe is in my nose,' she often said to those who admired her cooking. Her sense of smell determined if she had the right mix of ingredients and whether it was salty enough. Her eyes, tongue, and fingers judged whether the food had cooked long enough. As she saw it, it took only twenty additional seconds for fish to go from tender and juicy to overcooked and dry. Having grown up eating her food, I developed a refined palate for how Shanghainese dishes should taste, as well as an eye for how a dish should appear – how thick or thin or long the meat or vegetables had been sliced, whether the dish glistened with just the right amount of oil or was soaking in nasty pools of it. Being in the kitchen with her was stressful. She was a perfectionist...

From *Where the Past Begins*, 2017 | Amy Tan (b.1952)

I need to tell you that it is possible to be very frightened of something, and for that thing to happen, and for it still to be okay. It's possible to have your worst fear realised, and to find there is joy and rhubarb and ginger on the other side.

I don't have panic attacks any more, really.

I drink decaf coffee from a silver pot, and buy fancy eggs, and I have enough space in my kitchen to put everything away properly, and the kitchen is small and sunny and I can see the new roses through the window. I cook every day.

I share this kitchen with one of my favourite people in the world, and every night I cook her exactly what she wants, and in exchange she listens to me complain about things and does all the washing up, and in this way we both get exactly what we need. I make her cookies and banana bread and lemon cake. Sometimes I cook something pointlessly elaborate to please myself: lobster-glazed broccoli for a random Tuesday, gochujang duck confit, a pie with a hundred tiny flowers and trailing vines and her name spelled out in Parmesan pastry Scrabble tiles. Sometimes she makes me pesto pasta and we eat it in front of the telly. Sometimes other people come for dinner – her friends, my friends, our friends – and we eat pancakes with pistachio cream, or honey-glazed pancetta steaks. Sometimes I go out. Sometimes I go dancing. Sometimes I sit on the balcony steps with a mug of tea, early, before anyone is awake and I can't believe how lucky I am.

From *Midnight Chicken* (*& other recipes*), 2019 | Ella Risbridger (b.1992)

Chapter 4

FRIENDS

FRIENDS

How to praise, how even to approach, friendship?

Joyce Carol Oates (b.1938)

The most holy bond of society is friendship

Mary Wollstonecraft (1759–1797)

Each friend represents a world in us, a world possibly not born until they arrive

Anaïs Nin (1903–1977)

Shu Hua spoke to me two nights ago in bed and asked if I would consent to make you a Blood Sister with us, and my spirit was full of joy ... you are certainly our sister already in soul, and it is fitting you should become one by the correct rites.

From *The Pool of Ch'ien Lung*, 1948 | Dorothea Hosie (1885–1959)

For the moment one says, 'I will be your friend,' and you accept it, it is an era quite as notable, and as much to be accounted of, as if it were the lover to whom one gave oneself, body and soul, for ever!

Geraldine Endsor Jewsbury (1812–1880) to Jane Welch Carlyle, 25 June 1845

There are women whose eyes lock momentarily in bars, across crowded rooms, in the street and, though they are strangers, they recognise each other. They go through that female summing up thing, the subliminal eyeflick, the quick flick from shoes to haircut, and for a second their eyes meet.

I could be friends with you, they think. There goes a fellow smoker, drinker, slut, slag, domestic failure, neurotic, whatever, they think. A fellow traveller, a soul mate, they think. Sometimes they leave it at that, a moment's wondering and speculation. They do not act upon that look and make friends.

But sometimes they do.

From *Women Talking Dirty*, 1995 | Isla Dewar (1946–1921)

Her old friend had come home. Sula. Who made her laugh, who made her see old things with new eyes, in whose presence she felt clever, gentle and a little raunchy. Sula, whose past she had lived through and with whom the present was a constant sharing of perceptions. Talking to Sula had always been a conversation with herself. Was there anyone else before whom she could never be foolish? In whose view inadequacy was mere idiosyncrasy, a character trait rather than a deficiency? Anyone who left behind that aura of fun and complicity? Sula never competed; she simply helped others to define themselves. Other people seemed to turn their volume on and up when Sula was in the room. More than any other thing, humor returned...

From *Sula*, 1973 | Toni Morrison (1931–2019)

Phone rang: Miss Sue from up the street wants to get some 'healing water' from a spring she has heard about. This spring used to be for whites only. Now, integrated. It is a trickle as big as a finger.

She comes to the door and Mama lets her in.

I love knowing that I come from a mother who had staunch woman friends her whole long life. That they shared adventures and tribulations and jokes. That they understood the history, social and otherwise, of something as odd as this segregated, now integrated, 'healing water.'

Diary entry, April 1983, from *Gathering Blossoms Under Fire*, 2022 | Alice Walker (b.1944)

We are friends for life. When we're together the years fall away. Isn't that what matters? To have someone who can remember with you? To have someone who remembers how far you've come?

Judy Blume (b.1938)

The companions of our childhood always possess a certain power over our minds which hardly any later friend can obtain.

From *Frankenstein*, 1818 | Mary Shelley (1797–1851)

My favourite seat was a smooth and broad stone, rising white and dry from the very middle of the beck, and only to be got at by wading through the water; a feat I accomplished barefoot. The stone was just broad enough to accommodate, comfortably, another girl and me, at that time my chosen comrade – one Mary Ann Wilson; a shrewd, observant personage, whose society I took pleasure in, partly because she was witty and original, and partly because she had a manner which set me at my ease. Some years older than I, she knew more of the world, and could tell me many things I liked to hear: with her my curiosity found gratification: to my faults also she gave ample indulgence, never imposing curb or rein on anything I said...

And where, meantime, was Helen Burns? Why did I not spend these sweet days of liberty with her? or was I so worthless as to have grown tired of her pure society? Surely the Mary Ann Wilson I have mentioned was inferior to my first acquaintance: she could only tell me amusing stories, and reciprocate any racy and pungent gossip I chose to indulge in; while, if I have spoken truth of Helen, she was qualified to give those who enjoyed the privilege of her converse, a taste of far higher things.

True, reader; and I knew and felt this: and though I am a defective being, with many faults and few redeeming points, yet I never tired of Helen Burns; nor ever ceased to cherish for her a sentiment of attachment, as strong, tender, and respectful as any that ever animated my heart. How could it be otherwise, when Helen, at all times and under all circumstances, evinced for me a quiet and faithful friendship, which ill-humour never soured, nor irritation ever troubled? But Helen was ill at present: for some weeks she had been removed from my sight...

From *Jane Eyre*, 1847 | Charlotte Brontë (1816–1856)

'Marilla,' she demanded presently, 'do you think that I shall ever have a bosom friend in Avonlea?'

'A – a what kind of friend?'

'A bosom friend – an intimate friend, you know – a really kindred spirit to whom I can confide my inmost soul. I've dreamed of meeting her all my life. I never really supposed I would, but so many of my loveliest dreams have come true all at once that perhaps this one will, too. Do you think it's possible?'

'Diana Barry lives over in Orchard Slope, and she's about your age. She's a very nice little girl...'

From *Anne of Green Gables*, 1908 | L M Montgomery (1874–1942)

Love and Friendship

Love is like the wild rose-briar,
Friendship like the holly-tree –
The holly is dark where the rose-briar blooms
But which will bloom most constantly?
The wild rose-briar is sweet in spring,
Its summer blossoms scent the air;
Yet wait till winter comes again
And who will call the wild-briar fair?

Then scorn the silly rose-wreath now
And deck thee with the holly's sheen,
That when December blights thy brow
He still may leave thy garland green.

Emily Brontë (1818–1848)

Alice and I are best friends. I've known her all my life...

I've got heaps of ordinary friends as well as my best friend Alice. Last birthday I invited three boys and three girls for a sleepover party. Alice was top of the list, of course. We were supposed to play out in the garden but it rained, so we all had a crazy game of football in the living room (well, not quite all – Alice wouldn't play and

Biscuits is rubbish at games). Someone broke my mum's wedding present Lladro lady and burst the cushion. My mum was so mad she wouldn't let any of them sleep over and sent them all home. Except for Alice.

I'm still allowed one-special-friend sleepovers so long as that special friend is Alice. So that's great great great because as I've probably said before, Alice is my very best friend.

I don't know what I'd do without her.

From *Best Friends*, 2004 | Jacqueline Wilson (b.1945)

The progress of the friendship between Catherine and Isabella was quick as its beginning had been warm, and they passed so rapidly through every gradation of increasing tenderness, that there was shortly no fresh proof of it to be given to their friends or themselves. They called each other by their Christian name, were always arm in arm when they walked, pinned up each other's train for the dance, and were not to be divided in the set; and if a rainy morning deprived them of other enjoyments, they were still resolute in meeting in defiance of wet and dirt, and shut themselves up, to read novels together.

From *Northanger Abbey*, 1817 | Jane Austen (1775–1817)

'Never break a date with a girl for a man' was one of our mottoes in a period when women's loyalty to women was – as it usually still is – subordinate to their possible relationships with men. We learned loyalty to women, pleasure in conversation with women, and enjoyment of the way in which we complemented one another in terms of our differences in temperament, which we found as interesting as the complementarity that is produced by the difference of sex. Throughout extraordinarily different career lines we have continued to enjoy one another, and although meeting becomes more difficult as we scatter in retirement, we continue to meet and take delight in one another's minds.

From *Blackberry Winter: My earlier years*, 1972 | Margaret Mead (1901–1978)

Ermengarde did not know why a lump came into her throat and her eyes felt as if tears were in them.

'Lavinia and Jessie are "best friends", she said rather huskily. 'I wish we could be "best friends".' Would you have me for yours? You're clever, and I'm the stupidest child in the school, but I – oh, I do so like you!'

'I'm glad of that,' said Sara. 'It makes you thankful when you are liked. Yes. We will be friends. And I'll tell you what' – a sudden gleam lighting her face – 'I can help you with your French lessons.'

From *A Little Princess*, 1905 | Frances Hodgson Burnett (1849–1924)

2 a.m. Feeling v emotional. At the door were Magda, Tom, Shazzer and Jude with bottle of champagne. They said to hurry up and get ready and when I had dried hair and dressed they had cleaned up all the kitchen and thrown away the shepherd's pie. It turned out Magda had booked a big table at 192 and told everyone to go there instead of my flat, and there they all were waiting with presents, planning to buy me dinner. Magda said they had had a weird, almost spooky sixth sense that the Grand Marnier soufflé and frizzled lardon thing were not going to work out.

From *Bridget Jones's Diary*, 1996 | Helen Fielding (b.1958)

When I am in the company of women… I relax about my attractiveness, in the broadest sense of that word. I feel accepted as I really am. I can eat garlic, reveal the fact that I'm wearing torn underwear, commiserate about certain ineptitudes. Most important, I can tell my stories and feel that they are heard and appreciated, because my listener is like me. ('Really??' she will say, 'Yes!!' I will answer, happy as a clam.)

Elizabeth Berg (b.1948)

I've occasionally been told by women I know that I'm a good friend. I'm pleased, and don't dare say that, in general, I tend not to put next to the word 'friend' adjectives that refer to a hierarchy of feelings or reliability…

…The problem is that it comforts us to have many friends – it makes us feel popular, loved, less alone. We therefore prefer to describe as 'friends' women with whom we have little or nothing in common, but with whom, if necessary, we fill a void: we spend an afternoon in a cafe, we drink a glass of wine, talking about nothing in particular. Never mind if later, at the first opportunity, we call them gossips, snakes, sour, touchy. The fact is a woman friend is as rare as a true love. The Italian word for 'friendship', *amicizia*, has the same root as the verb 'to love', *amare*, and a relationship between friends has the richness, the complexity, the contradictions, the inconsistencies of love. I can say, without fear of exaggeration, that love for a woman friend has always seemed of a substance very similar to my love for the most important man in my life.

From the *Guardian*, 25 August 1981 | Elena Ferrante (b.1943), translated by Ann Goldstein

It's good, you know, when you've got a woman who is a friend of your mind.

Toni Morrison (1931– 2019)

Friendship is something to be built up carefully, by people with leisure. It is an art, nature does not enter into it.

From *The Pursuit of Love*, 1945 | Nancy Mitford (1904–1973)

In Caroline, Miss Keeldar had first taken an interest because she was quiet, retiring, looked delicate and seemed as if she needed someone to take care of her. Her predilection greatly increased when she discovered that her own way of thinking and talking was understood and responded to by this new acquaintance, She had hardly expected it. Miss Helstone, she fancied, had too pretty a face, manners and voice too soft, to be anything out of the common way in mind and attainments; and she very much wondered to see the gentle features light up archly to the *réveillé* of a dry sally or two risked by herself; and more did she wonder to discover the self-won knowledge treasured, and the untaught speculations working in that girlish, curl-veiled head. Caroline's instinct of taste, too, was like her own : such books as Miss Keeldar had read with the most pleasure were Miss Helstone's delight also. They held many aversions too in common, and could have the comfort of laughing together over works of false sentimentality and pompous pretension...

Caroline, she found, felt the value of true ore, and knew the deception of flashy dross. The minds of the two girls being toned in harmony, often chimed very sweetly together.

From *Shirley*, 1849 | Charlotte Brontë (1816–1856)

My God, I love to think of you, Virginia, as my friend. Don't cry me an ardent creature or say, with your head a little on one side, smiling as though you knew some enchanting secret: 'Well, Katherine, we shall see...' But pray consider how rare it is to find someone with the same passion for writing that you have.

Katherine Mansfield (1888–1923) to Virginia Woolf, 24 June, 1917

The truth is, I suppose, that one of the conditions unexpressed but understood of our friendship has been precisely that it is almost entirely founded on quicksands. It has been marked by curious slides & arrests; for months I've heard nothing of her; then we have met again upon what has the appearance of solid ground. We have been intimate, intense perhaps rather than open; but to me at any rate our intercourse has always been interesting & mingled with quite enough of the agreeable personal element to make one fond - if that is the word - as well as curious.

Diary entry, 18 February 1919 | Virginia Woolf (1882–1941) on Katherine Mansfield

So closely have been our lives, our purposes and experiences that, separated, we have a sense of incompleteness - united, such strength of self-assertion that no ordinary obstacles, difficulties or dangers appear to us as insurmountable.

Elizabeth Cady Stanton (1815–1902) to Susan B. Anthony

It's the friends you can call up at 4 a.m. that matter

Marlene Dietrich (1901–1992)

A friend is someone you can call in the middle of the night when your man is gone, or you wish he would go, or you suspect your cellulite is winning – or even just to prove to yourself that there is someone you can call in the middle of the night.

From *Vogue*, August 1981 | Anne Beatts (1947–2021)

Who can know the outer ranges of friendship? I am tempted to say that no one can live without it. It seems to me that trying to live without friends is like milking a bear to get cream for your morning coffee. It is a whole lot of trouble, and then not worth much after you get it.

From *Dust Tracks on a Road*, 1942 | Zora Neale Hurston (1891–1960)

I do, indeed, adopt you, dearest Mrs. Hoare, as a 'friend upon paper' – a true and dear friend! My best and most congenial habits of association and intercourse have so begun: and I do not think I have ever lost one, who has so taken to me and to whom I have so taken.

Mary Russell Mitford (1787–1855) to Mrs Hoare, 1853

Your letters are certainly like drinks of fine cold spring water on a hot day – They have a spark of the kind of fire in them that makes life worthwhile – That nervous energy that makes people like you and I want and go after everything in the world – bump our heads on all the hard walls and scratch our hands on all the briars – but it makes living great – doesn't it – I'm glad I want everything in the world – good and bad – bitter and sweet – I want it all and a lot of it too – Your letter makes me think that life is almost as good to you as it is to me.

From *Lovingly, Georgia*, 1990, Georgia O'Keefe (1887–1986) to Anita Pollitzer, 1915

A fortyish movie producer I'll call Samantha Jones walked into Bowery Bar, and, as usual, we all looked up to see whom she was with. Samantha was always with at least four men, and the game was to pick out which one was her lover...

We all admired Sam. First of all, it's not that easy to get twenty-five-year-old guys when you're in your early forties. Second, Sam is a New York inspiration. Because if you're a successful single woman in this city, you have two choices: You can beat your head against the wall trying to find a relationship, or you can say 'screw it' and just go out and have sex like a man. Thus: Sam...

We all sat back smugly, sipping tea, like we were members of some special club. We were hard and proud of it, and it hadn't been easy to get to this point...

From *Sex and the City*, 1996 | Candace Bushnell (b.1958)

Sometimes, while they sat on folding chairs underneath the big tree out front, watching the children play, the mothers argued with each other, screaming and shaking, while we children stood up and stared at them, but we never knew what had happened. Sometimes there were whispers of an affair, one of the women alone with one of the men, but the truth was denied us. A day or two later, one of the mothers sent one of the girls through the hallways with flowery, Scotch-taped notes of apology. These were delivered into tiny hot kitchens where blazing ovens held turkey, rib roasts, legs of lamb, the boiling vegetables sent tears rushing down the windows' glass. Often, the tears belonged to the woman setting the table, the quickly read note dropped on the dishes, we daughters overwhelmed by someone else's mother crushing us in her arms, her wet cheek stuck to our foreheads.

They cut and dyed one another's hair, and lent each other clothes, milk, slipcovers, curtains, and a ton of cigarettes. They ran back and forth over the roof from one apartment to the next when the children were sick, carrying alcohol for fever rubdowns, cod liver oil and Ace bandages and squares of flannel to press Musterole to our chests. Sometimes they delivered the big red encyclopaedia everyone borrowed for school reports, or baby food jars filled with whiskey that they mixed in our milk to ease our coughs.

They lent each other table money even if it meant hocking their wedding rings at the pawnbroker's, and if they met one another on the roof at dusk, looking for their husbands who were late again, they never made mention of it...

From 'Friendship's Gift' in *Between Friends*, 1994, edited by Mickey Pearlman | Christine O'Hagan (b.1953)

What are friends for, my mother asks,
A duty undone, a visit missed,
casserole unbaked for sick Jane.
Someone has just made her bitter.

Nothing. They are for nothing, friends,
I think. All they do in the end –
they touch you. They fill you like music.

Rosellen Brown (b.1939)

This is where I come to the part about friendship, for I am convinced that we could not have lived this life together as well as we did for as long as we did, nor seen it come to its peaceful and dignified conclusion, without the help of our friends...

Friends. So many times over the years, particularly in the last months, I heard them say the words, 'I feel so helpless. I don't know what to do.' I even said them myself. Yet when I look back over all these years and months and days, I see them coming in ripples, in waves, a creative wave of helping hands and hearts, reaching out, supporting, caring for us and about us, not always the same people, some going out of our ken for one reason or another and others coming in to take their place, still a constant, steadying presence in our lives, so manifest in what they did and said and gave to us over so many years.

These friends became our extended family throughout these years...

From 'Ringing the Net' in *Between Friends*, 1994, edited by Mickey Pearlman | Susan Kenney (b.1941)

Dear Friend

I turn to you, who have known pain and fear
And failure and despair, and in your eyes
I read companionship; and though your cloak
Be threadbare, half of it is mine
You are my friend.

Lilla Cabot Perry (1848–1933)

To her Lepidina, greetings
On the 3rd day before the Ides of September, sister, for the day of the celebration of my birthday, I give you a warm invitation to make sure that you come to us, to make the day more enjoyable for me by your arrival, if you come. Give my greetings to

your Certalis. My Aelius and my little son send you greetings. I shall expect you, sister. Farewell, my dearest soul, as I hope you prosper and hail.

Claudia Severa, *wife of a Roman garrison commander in northern England*, to Sulpicia Lepidina, c.100AD

This Little Bag

This little bag I hope will prove
To be not vainly made –
For, if you should a needle want
It will afford you aid.
And as we are about to part
'Twill serve another end,
For when you look upon the Bag
You'll recollect your friend.

Jane Austen (1775–1817)

How to describe my friend Pam? We met in childbirth class: she was having her fourth daughter, I was having my first son. On Christmas Eve she called from the hospital to say her baby was born; I immediately went into labor. Pam went to Brandeis and NYU film school before she married a divorced pediatrician at twenty-three and had a set of twins. The year her youngest son was born she was thirty, trying to finish a master's thesis in fiction at Boston university. She still hasn't finished that thesis. When a magazine offers to rent me the car of my dreams and pay expenses if I'll reprise a currently topical cinematic road trip with a female friend, I invite Pam. She has to call nine mothers before she finds someone to fill in as soccer coach and drive the girls' team, all the way to Sudbury. This isn't Thelma and Louise, this is Escape of the Suburban Mothers. We're like two animals let out of a cage: we don't know what to do first.

From 'Road Trip' in *Between Friends*, 1994, edited by Mickey Pearlman | Jayne Anne Phillips (b.1952)

Mine own Crow, harm not yourself for bootless help, but show a good example to comfort your dolorous yokefellow.

Although we have deferred long to represent to you our grieved thoughts, because we like full ill to yield you the first reflection of misfortunes, whom we have always rather sought to cherish and comfort, yet knowing now that necessity must bring it to your ears and nature consequently must move both grief and passions in you, we resolve no longer to smother either care for your sorrow or the sympathy of our grief for his loss.

Elizabeth I (1533–1601) to Lady Norris on the death of her son, 22 September 1597

I have always measured my life by the lives of my best women friends. In seventh grade, when it became time for Susan to begin thinking about men, it was time for me also to begin considering a personal life. My sense of order has come from sharing a well-considered point of view. If in high school Kathy considered so-and-so was crazy for befriending so-and-so, it was in fact a truth. There is nothing as comforting as knowing two opinions are right, to hell with what everyone else thinks.

Maybe, then, what I am missing these days are those complete and trusting alliances...

I am afraid of being guarded around other women, and I am afraid of moving on from friends when they no longer suit my life plans.

I know women's friendships have their ups and downs. It isn't always Bette Midler and Barbara Hershey sunlit and loving in Beaches. But it isn't the jungle red frenzy of The Women either...

Over the past year I've made contact again with the friend who had stopped speaking to me. At first, like any splintered relationship, our contact was very delicate, A passing hello at a party, a dinner where at least three other mutual friends were present. And every time I thought to myself this is too difficult, women's friendships should be easy, I realized I didn't want to stop trying because the truth was her friendship was irreplaceable.

Now we chat around once a month about her love life or my mordant insecurities. We even had a lunch alone together in California across the room from John Travolta and his new baby. As we sat there checking out the baby, the wife, and the manager, there was a moment when all the murky feelings went away and we were 'girlfriends' in the best sense of the word, giggling slightly and defiantly secure in our mutual affection.

Great friendships with women are some of life's most difficult and caring intimacies. If I work harder at them, I hope to have them forever.

From 'The Ties that Wound' in *Between Friends*, 1994, edited by Mickey Pearlman |
Wendy Wasserstein (1950–2006),

Before they were mothers
Leto and Niobe
had been the most
devoted of friends

Sappho (c.610–c.570BC)

In old age I see more of my friends than my family. My two grannies lived with mum and dad until the day they died, squashed together in one room – they fought like cat and dog and must have driven my parents insane. I am independent, and my daughters have busy family units to which I am an occasional visitor. They, especially Ellie Jane, are there if I need them, but up till now I seldom have. It is a part of Nature that animals leave the nest when they are mature and set up new nests, but deserted parent birds still fly or float around with their mates. As do I.

During my marriages I neglected my friends...

Diary entry, July 2019, from *Old Rage*, 2022 | Sheila Hancock (b.1933)

I mean I was quite proud of Dorothy the way she stood up for my reputation. Because I really think there is nothing so wonderful as two girls when they stand up for each other and help each other a lot.

From *Gentlemen Prefer Blondes*, 1925 | Anita Loos (1889–1991)

Dearest Ruth,
The problem with you being ill is that when I don't hear from you I fret and worry, almost certainly completely needlessly. This must be very annoying for you, knowing that people are thinking, 'ooh, I wonder if she's ok' when you are probably just busy or can't be arsed to email. So I'll assume you're okay and moan about myself instead.

India Knight (b.1965) to Ruth Picardie, email, 11 March 1997

...Please carry on moaning – I hate it when people can only talk about cancer. I know exactly what you mean about house being too small... – however big one's house, you always expand to over fill it...

Ruth Picardie (1964–1997) to India Knight, email, 13 March 1997

Dearest Ruth, Are you actually IN the hospital? Or at home? Oh arse. I can't send you weepy why-oh-why missives every day, so I am going to carry on as normal, and if I bore the pants off you in the process pls write and tell me. I suppose now you can safely carry out the 'I never liked you and you small of wee' school of 'pal'-shedding.

India Knight (b.1965) to Ruth Picardie, email, 5 June 1997

Dearest India,
A million apologies for my silence. I have become (even more of) a bitter, angry, envious depressed old cow who can't be bothered even to read her e-mails...

Ruth Picardie (1964–1997) to India Knight, email, 10 June 1997

'You are my best friend and I am so reluctant to let you go. I've been putting off thinking about you dying because I just don't know how my life will be without you. We have done so many hugely important and amazingly trivial things together – you are the diary I never kept.'

Email from another friend, Jenny Dee to Ruth Picardie (1964–1997), *Before I Say Goodbye*, Penguin, 1998

Diana was of the generation of Britons who regarded all Germans as enemies, and she and her sister-in-law held each other at arm's length for a number of years before becoming neighbours in Italy. They had not, in truth, appreciated each other in the past. Diana was always polite, but every now and again she would unconsciously refer to Germans as 'Huns', at which point Marta, whose father had been interned by the Nazis as a Communist, would raise an eyebrow. Had they not been fellow foreigners in a provincial town, it was unlikely that they would have become friends. Yet late in life each discovered that despite their differences in nationality, lifestyle and politics they could both like and admire each other. What they had in common was not just happenstance, but a steely sense of morality and generosity that had evolved into a reluctant warmth.

'Marta is not exactly my cup of tea,' Diana confessed to Ruth, 'but despite her ego, she is a very decent sort'; whereas Marta said to Ruth, 'She has views that bring me out in humps, yet her heart is in the right place.'

To both, Ruth said, 'It's more important to see the good in people than to focus on small differences.'

From *The Three Graces*, 2023 | Amanda Craig (b.1959)

Here for the first time the speaker lifted his gaze from the bowl of marigolds, let it travel slowly round the table, and brought it to rest on the Warden's intent face.

'Will you let me say, here and now, that the one thing which frustrated the whole attack from first to last was the remarkable solidarity and public spirit displayed by your college as a body. I think that was the last obstacle that X expected to encounter in a community of women. Nothing but the very great loyalty of the Senior Common Room to the College and the respect of the students for the Senior Common Room stood between you and a most unpleasant publicity. It is the merest presumption in me to tell you what you already know far better than I do; but I say it, not only for my own satisfaction, but because this particular kind of loyalty forms at once the psychological excuse for the attack and the only possible defence against it.'

'Thank you,' said the Warden. 'I feel sure that everybody here will know how to appreciate that.'

From *Gaudy Night*, 1935 | Dorothy L Sayers (1893–1957)

'Oh, you darling!' Miss LaFosse leaned forward impulsively and kissed her again, and there, right there on Miss Pettigrew's clasped hands, fell two drops of water and two more were trickling down her cheeks, Miss Pettigrew flushed a delicate pink.

'I have not,' said Miss Pettigrew in humble excuse, 'had much affection in my life.'

'Oh, you poor thing,' said Miss LaFosse gently. 'I've always had such a lot.'

'I'm glad,' said Miss Pettigrew simply,

After that they were friends and Miss La Fosse, tactfully, ignored the tears.

From *Miss Pettigrew Lives For a Day*, 1938 | Winifred Watson (1906–2002)

There is nothing like puking with somebody to make you into old friends.

From *The Bell Jar*, 1963 | Sylvia Plath (1932–1963)

The British anthropologist Robin Dunbar thinks we can't maintain stable social relationships with more than about 150 people. I don't think my active social circle is as big as that, but there are quite a few people I meet for coffee, lunch or drinks, just because I like them.

Friends are something else. Friends are the people who are there in the middle of the night when your heart has been broken. They are the people who will offer you a room when your flat is flooded, or when you're so exhausted that you have decided to buy yourself some time off and rented your flat out on Airbnb. Friends are the people who cook food for your parties, because they know you hate cooking, or who open their hearts and homes to you, because your weird illness has come back and the doctors can't seem to do anything about it, and nor can they, but at least they can offer you some company, some home-cooked food and some nice wine.

It goes without saying that you will do the same, or something similar, for them. Because that's the other thing about friendship: it's equal. It's reciprocal. It's give and take.

From *The Art of Not Falling Apart*, 2018 | Christina Patterson (b.1963)

Here in this cabin, twenty-five hundred miles from Louisiana, and many years from my girlhood, if I close my eyes and concentrate, I can smell my mother and the Ya-Yas, It's as though my own body keeps the scent of the Ya-Yas simmering on some back burner, and at most unexpected moments, the aroma rises up and joins with the fragrance of my current life to make a new-old perfume. The soft aroma of old worn cotton from a linen chest; the lingering smell of tobacco on an angora sweater; Jergens hand lotion, sautéed green peppers and onions; the sweet, nutty smell of peanut butter and bananas; the oaken smell of good bourbon; a combination of lily of the valley, cedar, vanilla, and somewhere, the lingering of old rose.

These smells are older than any thought. Mama, Teensy, Necie, and Caro, each one of them had an individual scent, to be sure. But this is the gumbo of their scents. This is the Gumbo Ya-Ya. This is the internal vial of perfume I carry with me everywhere I go.

The four of their scents were in key. Their very bodies harmonized together.

Surely this made it easier for them to forget things and forgive each other, not to have to constantly 'work' on things, the way we do now. This has never happened to me with a group of women. It is hard for me to even imagine. Yet I have seen it. I have smelled it.

From *Divine Secrets of the Ya-Ya Sisterhood*, 1996 | Rebecca Wells (b.1952)

With work memos out of the way, I can get to the real e-mails, the ones that matter: messages from friends, jokes and stories handed around the world like sweets. If it's really true what they say, that mine is the time-famished generation, then e-mail is our guilty snack, our comfort food. It would be hard to explain how much sustenance I get from my regular correspondents. There's Debra, my best friend from college, now mother of two and a lawyer with Addison Pope. just across the way from the Bank of England and about ten minutes' walk from Edwin Morgan Forster. Not that I ever get down there to see her. Might as well work on Pluto. And then there's Candy. Foul-mouthed fellow fund manager, World Wide Web whizz and proud export of Rockaway, New Jersey, Candace Marley Stratton. My sister-in-arms and a woman in the vanguard of the latest developments in world corsetry ...

Candy sits right over there, next to the pillar, fifteen feet away, and yet we scarcely exchange more than a few words out loud during an average day. On screen, though, we're in and out of each other's minds like old-fashioned neighbours.

From *I Don't Know How She Does It*, 2003 | Allison Pearson (b.1960)

Regardless of where we are in the world, we will either talk or be together on our birthday [April 24]. She is sentimental that way, and we are family.

She is a woman I feel attached to, and I love her and appreciate what she has done with her life. She is an inspiration to me because whatever baggage she carries around with her as a Taurus is the baggage I carry myself.

May she shine forever, because then I and others like us can see ourselves.

From *My Lucky Stars: A Hollywood Memoir,* 1995 | Shirley MacLaine (b.1934) on Barbra Streisand

Hope and I became really close friends during the summer of 1968, when I came back to New York from Heidelberg for a week to watch my grandmother die of cancer. I walked into her office and felt I had come home. It was a sunny room with thick gold carpeting and a large desk covered with trinkets, photographs, flowers. People were always sending Hope flowers.

'Let me look at you,' Hope said. I looked at her while she looked at me, and it was love at first sight. Hope was plump, gray-haired, and gave off warmth like an open fireplace. Her presence had a way of smoothing out all one's lumps and bumps, of making one feel mellow. My mother always made me feel nervous: Hope made me feel calm.

From *How to Save Your Own Life*, 1977 | Erica Jong (b.1942)

The two girls were silent for some time, both gazing into the fire. Cynthia spoke first:

'I wish I could love people as you do, Molly!'

'Don't you?' said the other, in surprise.

'No. A good number of people love me, I believe, or at least they think they do; but I never seem to care much for anyone, I do believe I love you, little Molly, whom I have only known for ten days, better than any one.'

From *Wives and Daughters*, 1866 | Mrs Gaskell (1810–1865)

This is what I miss, Cordelia: not something that's gone, but something that will never happen. Two old women giggling over their tea.

From *Cat's Eye*, 1988 | Margaret Atwood (b.1939)

Now that women's self-vision is changing, we are thinking again about the life of Marilyn Monroe. Might our new confidence in women's existence with or without the approval of men have helped a thirty-six-year-old woman of talent to stand on her own? To resist the insecurity and ridicule?...

Most of all, we wonder if the support and friendship of other women could have helped... In films, photographs, and books, even after her death as well as before, she has been mainly seen through men's eyes.

We are too late. We cannot know whether we could have helped Norma Jean Baker or the Marilyn Monroe she became. But we are not too late to do as she asked. At last, we can take her seriously.

'Marilyn Monroe: The Woman Who Died Too Soon', 1972, from *Outrageous Acts and Everyday Rebellions*, 1984 | Gloria Steinem (b.1934)

My Beautiful, Fair-Haired Countess,

I am not personally acquainted with you, but I have heard Franz talk about you, and have seen you myself. I believe that, after that, I may without folly tell you that I love you, that you seem to me the only beautiful, estimable, and truly noble star which I have seen shining in the patrician sphere. You must indeed be very attractive, since I forgot your being a countess. But now you are to my eyes the real type of the fantastic princess, artistic, loving, and noble in her ways, language and dress, like the daughters of kings in poetic times.

George Sand (1804–1876) to the Countess Marie d'Agoult, May 1835

We have drunk wine and discussed literature
Our hearts have beat together
With the same emotions.
Softly we sing together the old song
'The Sunlight in the Pass.'
The sorrow of parting will follow our horses' feet.
The melancholy of farewell
Surrounds the city like a river
Iron strokes, silver curves, your couplets
Are limitless in their meanings
Take care of yourself. We can have no confidence
That one day we will see each other again.
We stand on the bridge, hand in hand.
The river and the evening clouds stretch away for a
thousand miles.

Qiu Jin (1895–1907) on the departure of her female friend Tzu-ying

The two ladies continued to the last devoted to each other, and if they had a difference of opinion, they discussed it in a particular walk where they could not be overheard, for as they felt themselves bound to give to the world, an example of perfect friendship, the slightest appearance of discord would have tarnished their reputation.

Caroline Hamilton (1777–1861) on Sarah Ponsonby and Lady Eleanor Butler, the Ladies of Llangollen

In their journey through life, women look for and find female companionship. Within their friendships they talk uninhibitedly with each other about the details of sex, about what they want and what they have in their love relationships. They talk about their fears, their hopes for the future, their fantasies. Since early childhood women have learned to be attentive listeners and good givers and this is evident in their friendships where they can give each other support, understanding, comfort, sympathy and advice...

Such is the positive, nurturing side of women's relationships. Women cooperate and support each other and give each other enormous pleasure. But women's positive feelings towards each other have a counterpart in equally powerful negative feelings. Women's relationships produce a rainbow of powerful emotions. The recent delight and recognition of the importance of women's relationships and the ideology of 'sisterhood is powerful' has, in some ways, served to obscure much of the pain in women's friendships. But as we can trust the importance and value of these relationships, we are then able to face the fact that they are not idyllic...

...Today women have the possibility of allowing each other differences, of supporting the choice to become mothers or not; of recognizing the differences in the lives of single women and women in couples. We have the opportunity to acknowledge our need for other women as well as our need for recognition and acceptance of our autonomous selves. This time around we can offer this to each other.

From *Bittersweet: Facing Up to Feelings of Love, Envy and Competition in Women's Friendships*, 1987 | Susie Orbach (b.1946) and Luise Eichenbaum (b.1952)

And thank you for my dear letter, which came on Saturday night, when all the world was still; thank you for the love it bore me, and for its golden thoughts, and feelings so like gems, that I was sure I gathered them in whole baskets of pearls!

Emily Dickinson (1830–1866) to Susan Gilbert, *who would become her sister-in-law as well as her friend*, February 1852

From *Together*

I wonder if you really send
Those dreams of you that come and go!
I like to say, 'She thought of me
And I have known it.' Is it so?

Though other friends walk by your side,
Yet sometimes it must surely be,
They wonder where your thoughts have gone,
Because I have you here with me.

And when the busy day is done
And work is ended, voices cease,
When every one has said good night,

In fading firelight, then in peace
I idly rest – you come to me
Your dear love holds me close to you.
If I could see you face to face
It would not be more sweet and true.

Sarah Orne Jewett (1849–1909) to honour Annie Fields, 1875

The three girls in the corners of the railway carriage stopped talking, as the train drew up in Wycombe station... two were old friends, who shared rooms together in town. Norah and Connie were a recognised couple. Con, who sold gloves in a big West-End establishment, was the wife and home-maker; Norah, the typist, was the husband, who planned little pleasure trips and kept the accounts and took Con to the pictures.

From *The Abbey Girls Win Through*, 1928 | Elsie J Oxenham (1880–1960)

I read your letter with dismay, Ellen – what shall I do without you? Why are we so to be denied each other's society? It is an inscrutable fatality. I long to be with you because it seems as if two or three days or weeks spent in your company would beyond measure strengthen me in the enjoyment of those feelings which I have so lately began to cherish. You first pointed out to me that way in which I am so feebly endeavouring to travel, and now I cannot keep you by my side. I must proceed sorrowfully alone.

Why are we to be divided? Surely, Ellen, it must be because we are in danger of loving each other too well – of losing sight of the Creator in idolatry of the creature...

Charlotte Brontë (1816–1855) to Ellen Nussey, 20 February 1837

Weary with a hard day's work – during which an unusual degree of Stupidity has been displayed by my promising pupils I am sitting down to write a few hurried lines to my dear Ellen. Excuse me if I say nothing but nonsense, for my mind is exhausted, and dispirited. It is a Stormy evening and the wind is uttering a continual moaning sound that makes me feel very melancholy – At such times, in such moods as these Ellen it is my nature to seek repose in some calm, tranquil idea and I have now summoned up your image to give me rest. There you sit, upright and still in your black dress and white scarf – your pale, marble-like face – looking so serene and kind – just like reality – I wish you would speak to me –. If we should be separated if it should be our lot to live at a great distance and never see each other again in old age how I should call up the memory of my youthful days and what a melancholy pleasure I should feel in dwelling on the recollection of my Early Friend Ellen Nussey!

If I like people it is my nature to tell them so and I am not afraid of offering incense to your vanity. It is from religion that you derive your chief charms and may its influence always preserve you as pure, as unassuming and as benevolent in thought and deed s you are now. What am I compared to you I feel my own utter worthlessness when I make the comparison. I'm a very coarse common-place wretch!

Charlotte Brontë to Ellen Nussey, October 1836

I write HONORA on the sparkling sand!
The envious waves forbid the trace to stay:
Honora's name again adorns the strand,
Again the waters bear their prize away!

So Nature wrote her charms upon thy face –

The cheek's bright bloom, the lip's envermeilled dye,
And every gay and every witching grace
That youth's warm hours and beauty's stores supply.

But Time's stern tide, with cold Oblivion's wave,
Shall soon dissolve each fair, each fading charm;
E'en Nature self, so powerful, cannot save
Her own rich gifts from this o'erwhelming harm.

Love and the Muse can boast superior power;
Indelible the letters they shall frame:
They yield to no inevitable hour,
But on enduring tablets write thy name.

Anna Seward (1742–1809) on Honora Sneyd

Dear Ellen
Emily [her sister Emily Brontë] suffers no more either from pain or weakness now. She never will suffer more in this world - she is gone after a hard short conflict. She died on Tuesday, the very day I wrote to you. ... She has died in a time of promise - we saw her torn from life in its prime - but it is God's will - and the place where she is gone is better than that she has left.

God has sustained me in a way I marvel at through such agony as I had not conceived. I now look at Anne and wish she were well and strong - but she is neither, nor is papa - Could you now come to us for a few days? I would not ask you to stay long. Write and tell me if you could come next week and what day and by what train - I would try to send a gig for you to Keighley - You will I trust find us tranquil.

C. Brontë

Try to come – I never so much needed the consolation of a friend's presence. Pleasure, of course, there would be none for you in the visit, except what your kind heart would teach you to find in doing good to others.

Charlotte Brontë to Ellen Nussey, 23 December 1848

'My dear Mrs Besant, I have so long wished to see you,' and I was standing with my hand in her firm grip, and looking for the first time in this life straight into the eyes of 'H.P.B.' I was conscious of a sudden leaping forth of my heart – was it recognition? – and then I am ashamed to say, a fierce rebellion, a fierce withdrawal, as of some wild animal when it feels a mastering hand... She talked of travels, of various countries, easy brilliant talk, her eyes veiled, her exquisitely moulded fingers rolling cigarettes incessantly... We rose to go, and for a moment the veil lifted, and two brilliant, piercing eyes met mine, and with a yearning throb in her voice: 'Oh, my dear Mrs Besant, if you would only come among us!' I felt a well-nigh uncontrollable desire to bend down and kiss her, under the compulsion of that yearning voice, those compelling eyes, but with a flash of the old unbending pride and an inward jeer at my own folly, I said a commonplace polite goodbye...

Annie Besant (1847–1933) on meeting the mystic and Theosophist Madame Blavatsky, 1889

You are part of the furniture of our souls – among the sacred things on the hearth.

George Eliot (1819–1880) to Elma Stuart, 12 January 1878

From *To Mrs M A at Parting*

Thy linger soul in me shall lie,
And all thy thoughts reveal;
Then back again with mine shall fly
And thence to me shall steal.
Thus still to one another tend;
Such is the sacred Name of Friend.

Thus our twin souls in one shall grow,
And teach the World new love,
Redeem the age and sex, and show
A flame Fate dares not move:
And courting Death to be our friend,
Our lives together too shall end.

Katherine Philips (1632–1664)

Cara, you and my own sister are the three women who are tied to my heart by a cord which can never be broken and which really pulls me continually... I love Cara and you with unchanged and unchangeable affection, and while I retain your friendship I retain the best that life has given me next to that which is the deepest and gravest joy in all human experience.

George Eliot (1819–1880) to Sara Hennell, 31 October 1854

What for years, you have been to me, how you have comforted my sorrows, peopled my loneliness, added to my happiness, and bettered in every way my whole nature, you can never know; and then – there will be so many, so many who will tell the same story: blessing you: that I felt impelled to speak now, when I could be heard.

Elma Stuart (c.1837–1903), first letter to George Eliot, January 1872

My heart has just been called back to the time when we used to sit with our arms around each other at the sunset hour & talk & talk of our friends & our homes & of ten thousand subjects of mutual interest until both our hearts felt warmer & lighter for the pure communion of spirit.

Antoinette Brown (1825–1921), ***abolitionist, and the first woman to be ordained as a mainstream minister in the USA*****, to Lucy Stone, 1852**

I don't know if I've had a past life, but somehow I feel Gayle and I have been connected before. When I met her, it was as if I met someone who mirrors exactly who I am. We share the same kind of hopes and desires. We get irritated over the same things. It's uncanny, but Gayle and I feel the same way about everything. I'm closer to her than anyone else in the world. She is my family. If anything ever happened to Gayle, it would be like losing a part of myself.

Oprah Winfrey (b.1954) on Gayle King, October 1989

Oh, if I could just get my arms around you! – And stay with you like that for hours, telling you so many things, & listening to all that you must have to say. – I love you very much, dear Anne, & I always shall.

– Ours was a perfect friendship – I knew it at the time – and it is still just as true. I would do anything in the world for you, & I know that you would for me. – And it doesn't matter if we never write, and never see each other, it is just the same, – except that it would be so nice to see each other!

Edna St. Vincent Millais (1892–1950) to Anne Gardner Lynch

She was all Sensibility and Feeling. We flew into each other's arms and after having exchanged vows of mutual Freindship [sic] for the rest of our Lives, instantly unfolded to each other the most inward secrets of our Hearts.

From *Love and Freindship*, 1790 | Jane Austen (1775–1817)

The visit was paid, their acquaintance re-established, their interest in each other more than re-kindled. The first ten minutes had its awkwardness and its emotion. Twelve years were gone since they had parted, and each presented a somewhat different person from what the other had imagined. Twelve years had changed Anne from the blooming, unformed girl of fifteen, into the elegant little woman of seven and twenty, with every beauty excepting bloom, and with manners as consciously right as they were invariably gentle; and twelve years had transformed the fine-looking, well-grown Miss Hamilton, in all the glow of health and the confidence of superiority, into a poor, infirm, helpless widow, receiving the visit of her former protégé as a favour; but all that was uncomfortable in the meeting had soon passed away, and left only the interesting charm of remembering former partialities and talking over old times.

From *Persuasion*, 1817 | Jane Austen (1775–1817)

Love, considered as an animal appetite, cannot long feed on itself without expiring... Friendship is a serious affection; the most sublime of all affections, because it is founded on principle, and cemented by time. The very reverse may be said of love. In a great degree, love and friendship cannot subsist in the same bosom; even when inspired by different objects they weaken or destroy each other, and for the same object can only be felt in succession. The vain fears and fond jealousies, the winds which fan the flames of love, when judiciously or artfully tempered, are both incompatible with the tender confidence and sincere respect of friendship.

From *A Vindication of the Rights of Women*, 1792 | Mary Wollstonecraft (1759–1797)

Meanwhile, I have caught up the threads of another friendship. Carrie Darling, when I was a young girl living in my own home, was my first intellectual friendship... Her friendship was of the utmost value to me: she stimulated all that was good in me – my love of learning and intellectual ambition, all my moral enthusiasm, and to some extent checked the vulgar materialism brought about by life in second-rate fashionable sets. Her personality had a certain distinction and charm... All this charm is gone... For thirteen years she has lived exclusively with inferiors... Poor clever Carrie! The whole week we spent in one long tale of married misery. To me the friendship is no longer invigorating. I have lived in some ways a more strenuously 'professional' life than she has, I am satisfied by love, and overburdened with friendships. But there is the supreme value of faithfulness... to drop a friend or be dropped degrades life – makes life seem a horrid morass where anyone may be left to die uncared for. All ties should be made in their degree secure – to be broken only by mutual consent and for very sufficient reasons.

Diary entry, 19 January 1896 | Beatrice Webb (1858–1943)

Mrs Thrale I like more and more. Of all the people I have ever seen since I came into this 'gay and gaudy world', I never before saw the person who so strongly resembles our dear father. I find the likeness perpetually; she has the same natural liveliness, the same general benevolence, the same rare union of gaiety and of feeling in her disposition.

And so kind is she to me! She told me at first that I should have all my mornings to myself, and therefore I have actually studied to avoid her, lest I should be in her way; but since the first morning she seeks me, sits with me, saunters with me in the park, or compares notes over books in the library; and her conversation is delightful; it is so entertaining, so gay, so enlivening, when she is in spirits, and so intelligent and instructive when she is otherwise, that I almost as much wish to record all she say, as all Dr. Johnson says.

Diary entry, 26 August 1778 | Fanny Burney (1752–1840)

Chapter 5
FASHION

FASHION

What country maiden charms thy heart,
However fair, however sweet,
Who has not learned by gracious Art
To draw her dress around her feet?

Sappho (c.610–c.570BC)

A woman who cuts her hair is about to change her life.

Coco Chanel (1883–1971)

Beautiful young people are accidents of nature, but beautiful old people are works of art.

Eleanor Roosevelt (1884–1962).

Give a girl the right pair of shoes and she'll conquer the world.

Marilyn Monroe (1926–1962)

When academics write about the language of clothes and describe the various messages that are encrypted in the garments, they seldom include in that vast vocabulary the word Rejoice! Clothing as a social system is supposed to emit various significant social and cultural signals but not those piercing feelings of joy that new clothes can bring to the wearer. In general I prefer, to those academic studies, the modest maxim of the children's writer, Noel Streatfield, who pointed out with simple but devastating precision, 'There is no doubt a new dress is a great help in all circumstances.'

From *The Thoughtful Dresser: The Art of Adornment, the Pleasures of Shopping, and Why Clothes Matter*, 2009 | Linda Grant (b.1951)

I can still remember an article I read in The Village Voice way back in the late 1980s about women shaving their heads as an act of both liberation and beauty. This was during the height of Sinéad O'Connor's popularity, and I suppose her iconic example gave permission to many other women to get rid of their hair as well. There were a series of photos of all these women with buzzed and bald head – and to me, they all looked stunning. I remember many of the interviewees using the word cleansing to describe the act, and one woman said that the ritual of shaving her head every week made her feel not only powerful and healthy but as if her life was suddenly in perfect order.

'Why I Cut Off All My Hair', *Oprah Daily*, 18 September 2024 | Elizabeth Gilbert (b.1969)

They led [Miss Pettigrew] into the bedroom. She had a quick bath while Miss Dubarry and Miss LaFosse concentrated on Miss LaFosse's wardrobe. She put on silk underclothes laid out for her by Miss LaFosse. She had never worn real silk underclothes in her life. At once they made her feel different. She felt wicked, daring, ready for anything. She left her hesitations behind with her home-made woollens.

'The psychology of silk underclothes has not yet been fully considered,' mused Miss Pettigrew happily.

She came back into the bedroom like a debutante. Even her legs, quite uncovered below the last short frill of lace, caused her no blushes...

'Can I look?' implored Miss Pettigrew.

'The mirror's waiting,' said Miss Dubarry.

Miss Pettigrew stood up. She turned round. She stared.

'No,' whispered Miss Pettigrew.

'Yes,' chorused the Misses Dubarry and LaFosse joyously.

'It isn't me,' gasped Miss Pettigrew.

'You in the flesh,' said Miss Dubarry.

'You as man intended,' encouraged Miss LaFosse.

Then they were both silent. This was a sacred moment. This was Miss Pettigrew's moment. They gave it the honour of silent admiration.

Miss Pettigrew stared. She caught the back of the chair for support. She felt faint. Another woman stood there. A woman of fashion: poised, sophisticated, finished, fastidiously elegant. A woman of no age. Obviously not young. Obviously not old. Who would care about age? No one. Not in a woman of that charming exterior. The rich, black velvet of the gown was of so deep and lustrous a sheen it glowed like colour. An artist had created it. It had the wicked, brilliant cut that made its wearer look both daring and chaste. It intrigued the beholder. He had to discover which. Its severe lines made her look taller. The ear-rings made her look just a little, well, experienced. No other word. The necklace gave her elegance. She, Miss Pettigrew, elegant...

She smiled. The woman smiled back, assured, composed. Where was the meek carriage, the deprecating smile, the timid shyness, the dowdy figure, the ugly hair, the sallow complexion? Gone. Gone under the magic of Du Barry's expert owner and manager.

From *Miss Pettigrew Lives For a Day*, 1938 | Winifred Watson (1906–2002)

You see a coat, you ask for it in your size. Not that coat, this coat and no other. And when they bring it to you, everyone turns around and looks, because the right coat, the right dress, the right hat is like a sneeze or an orgasm, there's no mistaking what has just happened.

From *The Thoughtful Dresser: The Art of Adornment, the Pleasures of Shopping, and Why Clothes Matter*, 2009 | Linda Grant (b.1951)

Then I saw a HAT – my dream hat – which I'd not dared to hope I'd be able to afford. There it perched on a stand: just the kind of coarsely woven straw, the exact shade of wine colour, the perfect dream of a hat – and only 16s 11d. I took it off the stand, tried it on and said, 'I'll take it please.' I think I rather shocked the assistant: she said, 'Won't madam try on further hats? They are all this season's models, and see – these are Hollywood styles!' Madam explained firmly that she hadn't a Hollywood face, and tried hard not to purr with delight as the pet of a hat was tucked into a green paper-bag.

Diary entry, 27 April 1942, from *Nella Last's War: A Mother's Diary 1939–45*, 1981 | Nella Last (1889–1968)

Far my favourite shop – but shop is too unworthy a word for such a shrine! – was the glamorous Maison St. Louis, where Miss Louise Piers plied her art, 'creating' (in this connection the word is fully justified) the lovely original hats for which she was famed – fascinating veiled Tricornes, small close-fitting helmets called 'Mercurys', and my own favourites, wide-winged hats... I remember the anticipatory thrill with which, three steps at a time, we ran up the stairs of Maison St. Louis, the agonies of temptation and indecision suffered in front of its enhancing mirrors, before, rapturously transfigured – for at that age the alchemical effect of a new hat was to be born anew – we finally emerged from that enchanting shop 'plumed like ostriches that wing the wind, more full of spirits than the month of May'.

'Our hats have gone to our heads! Our hats have gone to our heads!' we used to sing as we came out.

From *Remember And Be Glad*, 1952 | Lady Cynthia Asquith (1887–1960)

Dress has never been at all a straightforward business: so much subterranean interest and complex feeling attaches to it... [a subject] with a flowery head but deep roots in the passions.

From *Collected Impressions*, 1950 | Elizabeth Bowen (1899–1973)

A Paris dress makes one feel capable of charming a pearl out of an oyster.

Jean Dawnay, *Dior fashion model* (1925–2016)

Last night I was again at the Ball...There were near twelve Hundred people there all as fine as Sattins [sic] and feathers could make them. I find my millinery and Hair dressing Talents of great use on these occasions, as literally since I came here I have not spent a shilling on either article, as some remains of last Winter's finery varied by my own hand have supplied me with caps and tuckers, and as to la frizure I was provident enough never to suffer the Maid I keep to dress me so constantly as to lose the power or arranging my own locks...

Betsy Sheridan (1758–1837), journal-letter to her sister Alicia, 5 January 1790

Burn up the corsets! ...No, nor do you save the whalebones, you will never need whalebones again. Make a bonfire of the cruel steels that have lorded it over your thorax and abdomens for so many years and heave a sigh of relief, for your emancipation I assure you, from this moment has begun.

From *What To Wear*, 1873 | Elizabeth Stuart Phelps Ward (1844–1911)

'Now I must look at you, Fanny,' said Edmund, with the kind smile of an affectionate brother, 'and tell you how I like you; and as well as I can judge by this light, you look very nicely indeed. What have you got on?'

'The new dress that my uncle was so good as to give me on my cousin's marriage. I hope it is not too fine; but I thought I ought to wear it as soon as I could, and that I might not have such another opportunity all the winter. I hope you do not think me too fine.'

'A woman can never be too fine while she is all in white. No, I see no finery about you, nothing but what is perfectly proper. I like those glossy spots. Has not Miss Crawford a gown something the same?'

From *Mansfield Park*, 1814 | Jane Austen (1775–1817)

I go into my room, and do up my hair exquisitely, in the style of the Empire, and don my white gown – the one of the portrait. It is a flowing gown, such as statues have, with sleeves which I turn up above the elbow, cut somewhat high in the back and lower in the neck, so as to show a little of the bust with a broad piece of Valenciennes falling over it. The loose folds of the dress are tied at the waist by a ribbon, and also tied below the bosom by two ribbons sewn together and tied in a simple knot. No gloves, no ornaments. I am charmed with myself. My white arms beneath the white wool, oh, so white! I am pretty; I am animated. Am I really in Nice?

Diary entry, 10 September 1874 | Marie Bashkirtseff (1858–1884)

I made a short cut for it and the next news was I was in a heap, on a lot of spikes, some fifteen feet or so below ground level, at the bottom of a bag-shaped game pit.

It is at these times you realise the blessing of a good thick skirt. Had I paid heed to the advice of many people in England, who ought to have known better, and did not do it themselves, and adopted masculine garments, I should have been spiked to the bone, and done for. Whereas, save for a good many bruises, here I was with the fulness of my skirt tucked under me, sitting on nine ebony spikes some twelve inches long, in comparative comfort, howling lustily to be hauled out.

From *Travels in West Africa*, 1897 | Mary Kingsley (1862–1900)

The business enthralled her. Not only the making of money enthralled her, but the actual life of the shop enthralled her. The people who came into the shop. Those women, now, whose sole interest in life was clothes, clothes, more and more clothes. Jane had often an entirely unbusiness-like impulse to beg them to stop buying. There was pathos in this urge for clothes. Mrs Mallet, for instance, with some secret flame burning inside that slender body and dark eyes - what did she keep dressing up for? All those clothes she bought - red, silver, black, white - what for? To play bridge with the same women in the same drawing-rooms? To dine with those same women plus husbands, talk a little on singularly unstartling topics, play more bridge and go home to sleep and a husband to whom her beauty was a commonplace? Was it for that that Mrs Mallet clothed herself so radiantly? It couldn't be. She, in her secret self, held some excitement, some desire or search. She waited - but for what? She herself probably did not know.

From *High Wages*, 1930 | Dorothy Whipple (1893–1966)

I was known as a great beauty because I had a knack for attracting publicity. I was always falling through a skylight or holding a camel, wearing evening dress.

Lady Diana Cooper (1892–1966)

Alison was a woman who seemed to fill a room, even when she wasn't in it. She was of an unfeasible size, with plump creamy shoulders, rounded calves, thighs and hips that overflowed her chair; she was soft as an Edwardian, opulent as a showgirl, and when she moved you could hear (though she did not wear them) the rustle of plumes and silks. In a small space, she seemed to use up more than her share of oxygen; in return her skin breathed out moist perfumes, like a giant tropical flower. When you came into a room she'd left – her bedroom, her hotel room, her dressing room backstage – you felt her as a presence, a trail. Alison had gone, but you would see a chemical mist of hairspray falling through the bright air. On the floor would be a line of talcum powder, and her scent – Je Reviens – would linger in curtain fabric, in cushions, and in the weave of towels. When she headed for a spirit encounter her path was charged, electric; and when her body was out on stage, her face – cheeks glowing, eyes alight – seemed to float still in the dressing-room mirror.

From *Beyond Black*, 2005 | Hilary Mantel (1952–2022)

The only real elegance is in the mind; if you've got that, the rest really comes from it.

From *Newsweek*, 10 December 1962 | Diana Vreeland (1903–1989),

I like being a woman, even in a man's world. After all, men can't wear dresses, but we can wear the pants.

Whitney Houston (1963–2012)

Happiness ran over like the jet from a sudden unexpectedly spurting little wave. Birthday and fine weather in conjunction: the omens were propitious.

Which of the two jumpers – the crimson, the fawn? The fawn to-day. The crimson heartened the lesser days, put a firm face upon them. It suited her, as they said. But today she could suit her clothes, provide the glow, fill out the shape, warm up texture and colouring. She pulled on her brown stockinette skirt, regretting, but without irritation to-day, the slight bagginess at knees and bottom; fastened a broad scarlet patent-leather belt. The belt was an object that had virtue in it. She had had it for two years. It was cracked, peeling a little. Within its compass she felt a certainty of individuality, like a seal set on her, and she loved it, liked to think of it lying coiled, secret and brilliant, in the top left-hand drawer...

She cast a glance at her figure in the long glass; but the image failed her, remained unequivocally familiar and utilitarian.

Nowadays a peculiar emotion accompanied the moment of looking in the mirror: fitfully, rarely, a stranger might emerge: a new self.

From *Invitation to the Waltz*, 1932 | Rosamond Lehmann (1901–1990)

The hamlet's fashion lag was the salvation of its wardrobes, for a style became 'all the go' there just as the outer world was discarding it, and good, little-worn specimens came that way by means of the parcels. The Sunday garment at the beginning of the decade was the tippet, a little shoulder cape of black silk or satin with a long, dangling fringe. All the women and some of the girls had these, and they were worn proudly to church or Sunday school with a posy of roses or geraniums pinned in front...

...Then there were the bustles, at first looked upon with horror, and no wonder! but after a year or two the most popular fashion ever known in the hamlet and the one which lasted longest. They cost nothing, as they could be made at home from any piece of old cloth rolled up into a cushion and worn under any frock. Soon all the women, excepting the aged, and all the girls, except the tiniest, were peacocking in their bustles, and they wore them so long that Edmund was old enough in the day of their decline to say that he had seen the last bustle on earth going round the Rise on a woman with a bucket of pig-wash.

This devotion to fashion gave a spice to life and helped to make bearable the underlying poverty. But the poverty was there...

From *Larkrise to Candleford*, 1945 | Flora Thompson (1876–1947)

The month of courtship had wasted: its very last hours were being numbered. There was no putting off the day that advanced – the bridal day; and all preparations for its arrival were complete. I, at least, had nothing more to do: there were my trunks, packed, locked, corded, ranged in a row along the wall of my little chamber: to-morrow, at this time, they would be far on their road to London: and so should I (D.V.), – or rather, not I, but one Jane Rochester, a person whom as yet I knew not ... Mrs. Rochester! She did not exist: she would not be born till to-morrow, some time after eight o'clock A.M.; and I would wait to be assured she had come into the world alive before I assigned to her all that property. It was enough that in yonder closet, opposite my dressing-table, garments said to be hers had already displaced my black stuff Lowood frock and straw bonnet: for not to me appertained that suit of wedding raiment, the pearl-coloured robe, the vapoury veil, pendent from the usurped portmanteau. I shut the closet, to conceal the strange, wraith-like apparel it contained; which, at this evening hour – nine o'clock – gave out certainly a most ghostly shimmer through the shadow of my apartment. 'I will leave you by yourself, white dream,' I said. 'I am feverish: I hear the wind blowing: I will go out of doors and feel it.'

From *Jane Eyre*, 1847 | Charlotte Brontë (1816–1855)

So, you have got high-heeled shoes (? I do not) think of having them yet a while I am so little, and wish to appear as Girlish as possible I wear my hair curled about my face in light curls friz'd at the bottom and turned at the ends. How have you yours? I have tied my black hat under the chin, as it looked shabby in its former state.

Dorothy Wordsworth (1771–1855) to Jane Pollard, 6/7 August 1787

I must go and buy a hat this afternoon, I think, and tomorrow a dress. I must get on with the transformation act.

From *Good Morning Midnight*, 1939 | Jean Rhys (1890–1979)

It is true that I take care of the way I dress; and, as for feathers, everyone wears them, and it would seem extraordinary not to wear them. Their height has been much curtailed since the end of the balls...

Marie Antoinette (1755–1793) to her mother, 17 March 1775

The dress must not hang on the body but follow its lines. It must accompany its wearer and when a woman smiles, the dress must smile with her.

Madeleine Vionnet, *designer* (1876–1975)

All this time I have forgotten a most important event that has befallen me, which is a grand epoch in a woman's life. I have had – what? Guess. An offer of marriage? Never a bit of it. No man of my acquaintance has been so far abandoned by Providence. A lover, then? Still less. I am in no humour for human valentines; but what I have had is actually a real Cashmere shawl given me last week!! And upon my honour, a great many disagreeable things might come upon me which I should not feel now that I can wrap myself around with this mysterious and almost unknown production. It was reading the memoirs of 'Madame Lafarge' which first inspired me with an ardent passion for the unknown article.

Geraldine Endsor Jewsbury (1812–1880) to Jane Welsh Carlyle

When she had first started spending weekends with the Horse People, Daisy had been forced to carve out a unique style for herself. She couldn't possibly buy fashionable dinner clothes so she became an old clothes aficionado, avoiding the antique-clothing boutiques with their exquisite garments which only a Bette Midler or a Streisand could afford; avoiding the almost-new shops which were crammed with last year's couture clothes, already dated; and avoiding as well the flea markets at which only a miracle could uncover a garment in good condition.

Her buys all came from London jumble sales in church halls that she found time to go to each time she visited Dani. There she specialized in unearthing English and French couture originals, preferably over forty years old, clothes that had been made in the great dressmaking decades of the twenties and thirties. She researched them after she brought them back in triumph, for nothing she owned had cost over thirty-five dollars.

Daisy led Kiki into the third bedroom of their apartment in which she kept her nonworking clothes hanging on a horizontal pipe which crossed one end of the room.

The two girls stood and contemplated the garments that hung there. 'It wouldn't be so hard if you only had regular clothes, like other people,' Kiki sighed.

'Ah... that... how right you are. But it's simply too expensive and too dull, although I admit it would make life easier,' Daisy replied.

'The Vionnet?' Kiki suggested.

'Too dressy,' Daisy said regretfully, fingering the pale violet satin dress, cut on the bias and dating from 1926. 'What do you think about the striped Lucien Lelong?'

'To be honest, I've never really liked it on you. Your essential wood nymphishness is not enhanced by zebra stripes, no matter how well done. How about the black velvet Chanel suit? It may be forty years old, but it looks as if it had been born yesterday,' Kiki answered.

'It's not the right time of year for black velvet, especially in bluegrass country.'

'Wait, wait, I see those Dove tea pajamas – you said they were around 1925? Just look, Daisy, cyclamen brocade and green satin with a black satin jacket – it's a smash!'

'They're Locust Valley maybe or Saratoga, but definitely not Middleburg.'

'So that lets out the white satin pajama suit from Revillon too?'

'Afraid so. Oh, rot!'

Kiki carefully pushed the hangers aside, sighing wistfully over Daisy's treasures – they were all too long for her, but she itched after them.

'Ah ha!' Daisy pounced. 'How could I have forgotten? Schiaparelli to the rescue, as usual.' Triumphantly she held up an ensemble from the late 1930s when the daring Schiaparelli was doing clothes which were four decades ahead of her time. There was a jacket in lettuce green tweed touched with sequins at the lapels, worn with a pair of corduroy pants in a darker shade of green. 'Just right, don't you think?'

'It's heaven – really a fuck-you number, as in 'Fuck you, Mrs. Short, I know it's tweed and I know it's sequins and I know you didn't think they can be worn together, but now you do.'

'In a nutshell. I really need this commission, so it's important to look as if I didn't.'

'Then you'd better take my fake emeralds again.'

'Emeralds with green sequins?'

'Especially with green sequins!'

From *Princess Daisy*, 1980 | Judith Krantz (1928 – 2019)

Vulgarity is a very important ingredient in life. I am a great believer in vulgarity – if it's got vitality. A little bad taste is like a nice splash of paprika. We all need a splash of bad taste – it's hearty, it's physical... No taste is what I am against.

Diana Vreeland (1903–1989)

At the moment she was standing in a fitting-room whither she had dragged a visitor who had come on private business of his own and was surveying herself in a wall-wide mirror with earnest criticism.

Like most of those people whose personality has to be consciously expressed in the things they create, she was a little more of a person, a little more clear in outline than is usual. She had no suggestion of over-emphasis, but she was a sharp, vivid entity, and when one first saw her the immediate thing one realized was that it had not happened before.

As she stood before the mirror considering her burgundy-red suit from every angle she looked about twenty-three, which was not the fact. Her slenderness was slenderness personified and her yellow hair, folded softly into the nape of her neck at the back and combed into a ridiculous roll at the front, could have belonged to no-one else and would have suited no other face.

It occurred to her visitor, who was regarding her with the detached affection of a relation, that she was dressed up to look like a female, and he said so affably.

She turned and grinned at him, her unexpectedly warm grey eyes, which saved her whole appearance from affectation, dancing at him happily.

'I am,' she said. 'I am, my darling. I'm female as a cartload of monkeys.'

From *The Fashion in Shrouds*, 1938 | Margery Allingham (1904–1966)

At Greenwich

The 13 April, Madame my good aunt, as humbly as is possible I recommend myself to your good grace. And I have received the pattern of clothes which the ladies wear around you which you sent me, for which I greatly thank you. Because I have long wished to know how the ornaments and clothing used there will fit me and now that I have tried them I am greatly contented with them. Hoping that it will be an easy enough thing for me to leave off my accustomed way of dressing when I find myself with you...

Mary Tudor (1496–1533) to Margaret of Austria, 1513

It was a fine morning and I decided to go shopping and get rid of my heavy headache in the fresh air, and I wanted to see if my dress had come in to a shop where a consignment was expected. I got a really beautiful one, a real 'dream dress', and by God my diary and I will be the only ones to know what I paid – eight guineas. I told my husband it was over £5 and he nearly had a fit. I felt peeved when I thought how little I'd ever spent on clothes, always making them myself till I got my two last coats tailored. He never realises the days of cheap remnants have gone, and he is so unobservant he never sees changing prices and supplies. It's a soft turquoise blue that blends perfectly with the russet of my coat. I thought at first it was too young but the shop girl said, 'It's exactly your dress in style and colours are never considered 'young'.' Silly old thing – I don't remember feeling so excited over a dress since I was a girl. Cliff will understand. Maybe I'll whisper my sin to him when he comes!

Diary entry, 30 October 1945, from *Nella Last's Peace*, 2008 | Nella Last (1889–1968)

Egg Lytton Gore sat in an arm-chair of modern design – faintly reminiscent of a dentist's chair, and watched exquisite snake-like young women with beautiful bored faces pass sinuously before her. Egg was principally concerned with endeavouring to appear as though fifty or sixty pounds was a mere bagatelle to pay for a dress.

Mrs Dacres, looking as usual marvellously unreal, was (as Egg put it to herself) doing her stuff.

'Now, do you like this? Those shoulder knots - rather amusing, don't you think? And the waistline's rather penetrating. I shouldn't have the red lead colour, though - I should have it in the new colour - Espagnol - most attractive - like mustard, with a dash of cayenne in it. How do you like Vin Ordinaire? Rather absurd, isn't it? Quite penetrating and ridiculous. Clothes simply must not be serious nowadays.'

'It's very difficult to decide,' said Egg. 'You see' - she became confidential - 'I've never been able to afford any clothes before. We were always so dreadfully poor. I remembered how simply marvellous you looked that night at Crow's Nest, and I thought, 'Now that I've got money to spend, I shall go to Mrs Dacres and ask her to advise me.' I did admire you so much that night.'

'My dear, how charming of you. I simply adore dressing a young girl. It's so important that girls shouldn't look raw - if you know what I mean.'

'Nothing raw about you,' thought Egg ungratefully. 'Cooked to a turn, you are.'

From *Three Act Tragedy*, 1935 | Agatha Christie (1890–1976)

Vivi Walker walked down the tree-lined drive at Pecan Grove to get the mail. She had been lying on the window seat in the den, reading a novel and listening to Barbra Streisand when she heard the mail truck turn around. At sixty-seven, she was still fit from playing tennis twice a week. She'd put on five pounds since she'd tried to quit smoking, but she could still have passed for a much younger women. Her legs, though not tan, were muscular and strong. Her subtly colored ash-blonde hair was cut in a French bob, and over it she wore an expensive black straw hat of the best weave, which she had bought thirty-five years ago. She wore linen shorts, a crisp white blouse, and tennis shoes. Her jewelry consisted of a single twenty-four-carat-gold bracelet, her wedding ring, and a pair of tiny diamond earrings. This was her summer uniform, and had been since anybody in Cenla could remember.

From *Divine Secrets of the Ya-Ya Sisterhood*, 1996 | Rebecca Wells (b.1952)

Prune only knew of two dressmakers, Miss Spice in Pontisbright and Edmund Norman in London and Paris. Because it was to be the greatest day in her life she had gone, not unnaturally, to Norman. She had told him everything about herself and left it to him. She had the height and figure of a model, and at the only school she had ever attended they had taught her how to walk, if little else. The rest of the miracle had been performed by Charlie Luke, who walked now a little behind her looking as if he knew it. Her dress was made of tailored cream, which flattered her skin and her hair, and her shoes and long gloves and little handbag were all fashioned from the palest milk chocolate, or something very like it in tint and texture. Round her throat she wore the jade necklace, which deepened rather than echoed the colour of her eyes, and in her hand was the flagrant posy for a lover which Old Harry had wound according to the ancient way.

She was so ecstatically happy that she glowed with it as if she wore a glory, and every man who set eyes on her that day remembered her for the rest of his life.

From *The Beckoning Lady*, 1955 | Margery Allingham (1904–1966)

I believe that happy girls are the prettiest girls.

Audrey Hepburn (1929–1993)

This was my style: the coloured tights, the vintage dresses, the hennaed hair. This style was the summation of the identity I had been trying to achieve through the various experiments all the way through my teens...

At sixteen and again at sixty you are at the age when you use clothes to discover new identities. To stand in front of the mirror and see a different person with each garment you put on; to explore all those possibilities, those various selves. The shock of the new is as it is in the beginning. Never go beige into that good night, there will be more than enough time for neutrals in the darkness of the grave.

From *The Thoughtful Dresser: The Art of Adornment, the Pleasures of Shopping, and Why Clothes Matter*, 2009 | Linda Grant (b.1951)

I can remember as though I wore it still my comfortable, ill-fitting flannel suit, and how the skirt was lighter than the coat through harder wear. My shabby hat, too broad about the brim, and my low-heeled shoes, fastened with a single strap. A pair of gauntlet gloves grasped in a grubby hand. I had never looked so youthful, I had never felt so old.

From *Rebecca*, 1938 | Daphne du Maurier (1907–1989)

'Everyone was angry with her when she cut her hair,' she said, 'but she did not care. 'It's nothing to do with anyone but myself,' she would say. And of course short hair was much easier for riding and sailing. She was painted on horseback, you know. A famous artist did it. The picture hung in the Academy. Did you ever see it?'

I shook my head. 'No,' I said. 'No.'

'I understood it was the picture of the year,' she went on, 'but Mr de Winter did not care for it, and would not have it at Manderley. I don't think he considered it did her justice. You would like to see her clothes, wouldn't you?' She did not wait for my answer. She led me to the little ante-room and opened the wardrobes, one by one.

'I keep her furs in here,' she said, 'the moths have not got to them yet, and I doubt they ever will. I'm too careful. Feel that sable wrap. That was a Christmas present from Mr de Winter. She told me the cost once, but I've forgotten it now. This chinchilla she wore in the evenings mostly. Round her shoulders, very often, when the evenings were cold. This wardrobe here is full of her evening clothes. You opened it, didn't you? The latch is not quite closed. I believe Mr de Winter liked her to wear silver mostly. But of course she could wear anything, stand any colour. She looked beautiful in this velvet. Put it against your face. It's soft, isn't it? You can feel it, can't you? The scent is still fresh, isn't it? You could almost imagine she had only just taken it off. I would always know when she had been before me in a room. There would be a little whiff of her scent in the room. These are her underclothes, in this drawer. This pink set here she had never worn. She was wearing slacks of course and a shirt when she died. They were torn from her body in the water though. There was nothing on her body when it was found, all those weeks afterwards.'

From *Rebecca*, 1938 | Daphne du Maurier (1907–1989)

Miss Silver herself added to the homely effect. His old Cousin Connie also wore her hair in a curled fringe after the fashion set by Queen Alexandra in the late years of the previous century. Aunt Collie's stockings were of a similar brand of black ribbed wool. For the rest, Miss Silver was herself – a little governessy person with neat features and a lot of mouse-brown hair very strictly controlled by a net. It being three o'clock in the afternoon, she was wearing a pre-war dress of olive-green cashmere with a little boned lace front, very fresh and clean. A pair of pince-nez on a fine gold chain was looped up and fastened on the left side by a bar brooch set with pearls. She also wore a row of bog-oak beads ingeniously carved, and a large brooch of the same material in the shape of a rose, with an Irish pearl at its heart. Nothing could have felt less like a visit to a private detective.

From *Pilgrim's Rest*, 1948 | Patricia Wentworth (1877–1961)

A pair of large blue eyes looked at her steadily above the green hand-woven hood. Flora pensively noted that they were fine eyes, and that the hood was the wrong green.

She said, persuasively, 'Do forgive me saying so, but I would love to see you in blue. Some shades of green are good, of course, but dull greens are very trying I always think. If I were you, I should try blue – something really well cut, of course, and very simple – but definitely blue. You try it, and see.'

Elfine made a brusque boyish movement, and said offhandedly, 'This way.'

She strode along the corridor with a long, swinging step, letting the hood fall back so that Flora could see the back of her unbrushed mane of hair; it might have been a good gold if it had been properly dressed and cared for. It all seemed deplorable to Flora.

'Here,' jerked Elfine, stopping in front of a closed door.

Flora thanked her so much, and Elfine, after another long stare at her, strode away.

'She will have to be taken in hand at once,' thought Flora. 'Another year, and there will be no doing anything with her, for even if she escapes from this place, she will only go and keep a tearoom in Brighton and go all arty-and-crafty about the feet and waist.

And sighing a little at the greatness of the task which she had set herself to perform, Flora rapped at Judith's bedroom door, and in reply to a muttered 'come in', entered...

Flora first took Elfine to Maison Viol, of Brass Street, in Lambeth, to have her hair cut. Short hair was just coming back into fashion, yet it was still new enough to be distinguished. M. Viol himself cut Elfine's hair, and dressed it in a careless, simple, fiendishly expensive way that showed the tips of her ears.

Flora then took Elfine to Maison Solide. M. Solide had dressed Flora for the last two years and did not despise her as much as he despised most of the women he dressed. His eyes widened when he saw Elfine. He looked at her broad shoulders and slim waist and long legs. His fingers made the gestures of a pair of scissors, and he groped blindly towards a roll of snow-coloured satin which a well-trained assistant put into his arms.

'White?' ventured Flora.

'But what else?' screamed M. Solide, ripping the scissors across the satin. 'It is to wear white that God, once in a hundred years, makes such a young girl.'

Flora sat and watched for an hour while M. Solide worried the satin like a terrier, tore it into breadths, swathed and caped and draped it. Flora was pleased to see that Elfine did not seem nervous or bored. She seemed to take naturally to the atmosphere of a world-famous dressmaker's establishment. She bathed delightedly in white satin, like a swan in foam. She twisted her neck this way and that, and peered down the length of her body, as though down a snow slope, to watch the assistants like busy black ants pinning and rearranging the hem a thousand feet below...

She [Flora] had done what she had hoped to do. She had made Elfine look groomed and normal, yet had preserved in her personality a suggestion of cool, smoothly blowing winds and of pine trees and the smell of wild flowers. She had conceived just such a change, and M. Viol and M. Solide, her instruments, had carried it out.

An artist in living flesh could ask for no more, and the auguries for the evening of the dance were good.

From *Cold Comfort Farm*, 1932 | Stella Gibbons (1902–1989)

[The Cranford ladies'] dress is very independent of fashion; as they observe, 'What does it signify how we dress here at Cranford, where everybody knows us?' And if they go from home, their reason is equally cogent, 'What does it signify how we dress here, where nobody knows us?' The materials of their clothes are, in general, good and plain, and most of them are nearly as scrupulous as Miss Tyler, of cleanly memory; but I will answer for it, the last gigot, the last tight and scanty petticoat in wear in England, was seen in Cranford – and seen without a smile.

From *Cranford*, 1853 | Mrs Gaskell (1810–1865)

We began to talk of Miss Matty's new silk gown. I discovered that it would be really the first time in her life that she had had to choose anything of consequence for herself: for Miss Jenkyns had always been the more decided character, whatever her taste might have been; and it is astonishing how such people carry the world before them by the mere force of will. Miss Matty anticipated the sight of the glossy folds with as much delights as if the five sovereigns, set apart for the purchase, could buy all the silks in the shop; and (remembering my own loss of two hours in a toyshop before I could decide on what wonder to spend a silver threepence) I was very glad that we were going early, that dear Miss Matty might have leisure for the delights of perplexity.

If a happy sea-green could be met with, the gown was to be sea-green: if not, she inclined to maize, and I to silver gray...

From *Cranford*, 1853 | Mrs Gaskell (1810–1865)

I've been critical of Zelie. She cut her hair and I miss it so much... My own hair is half in tiny pigtails. I'm slowly taking out my dreadlocks. As Angela said: It's time. That's the only correct answer. It feels good to get to know my hair again. So springy and so fine! Where does it come from? This soft springy hair?

Diary entry, 11 November 1998, from *Gathering Blossoms Under Fire*, 2022 | Alice Walker (b.1944)

When I was a teenager, most arguments with my mother were about clothes. She was baffled by what it was inside myself that I was expressing outside of myself. She could no longer reach or recognize me. And that was the whole point. I was creating a persona that was braver than I actually felt. I took the risk of being mocked on buses and on the streets of the suburb in which I lived. The secret message that lurked in the zips of my silver platform boots was that I did not want to be like the people doing the mocking...

If we cannot at least imagine we are free, we are living a life that is wrong for us.

From *The Cost of Living*, 2018 | Deborah Levy (b.1959)

She had a few handsome dresses left – survivals of her last phase of splendour. ... as she spread them out on the bed, the scenes in which they had been worn rose vividly before her. An association lurked in every fold: each fall of lace and gleam of embroidery was like a letter in the record of her past. She was startled to find how the atmosphere of her old life enveloped her... She put back the dresses one by one, laying away with each some gleam of light, some note of laughter, some stray waft from the rose shores of pleasure.

From *The House of Mirth*, 1905 | Edith Wharton (1862–1937)

Rosy [Carita, co-founder of the eponymous post-war Paris hair salon] in her black sheath dress (the one she had just changed into) was more than lovely and her versatility gave her added charm. She slipped into a sealskin coat as black as her lovely hair, and exclaimed:

'I want to drive you home in my new car!'

At the wheel of her open Mercedes, the wind streaming through her hair and yet, by some miracle not appearing in any way to disarrange a single wisp, she looked like a young goddess of speed. 'Your hair?' I queried, raising my voice to make myself heard above the noise of the traffic. 'Doesn't it get tangled?' She laughed. 'No!' she answered. 'I could do a thousand kilometres like this. Not a hair would be out of place. Every worry, every attack of the spleen can be immediately got rid of by jumping into a fast car and driving off. I love fast cars. I used the first money I ever made to buy one.'

Now that she was in her element, darting in and out of the traffic, finding short cuts, increasing speed along the tree-lined embankment mysterious with reflected lights, she never stopped babbling away. I wondered to what extent high spirits and creation are kindred gifts. There is a youthful eagerness about these people who mould the appearance and shape and clothes of women, a bubbling and babbling of ideas, a serious light-heartedness, a joyful feeling that they are as much a part of the Paris scene as the chestnut-trees and the bridges over the Seine, and there is that rich rewarding of their talents that adds to their confidence and proves to them that they are leaders.

From *The Dream Makers*, 1961 | Mrs Robert Henrey (1906–2004)

When I went to bed, I stared earnestly at my face in the glass. Was I really good-looking? Honestly, I couldn't say I thought so! I hadn't got a straight Grecian nose, or a rosebud mouth, or any of the things you ought to have. It is true that a curate once told me that my eyes were like 'imprisoned sunshine in a dark, dark wood'– but curates always know so many quotations, and fire them off at random. I'd much prefer to have Irish blue eyes than dark green ones with yellow flecks! Still, green is a good colour for adventuresses.

I wound a black garment tightly round me, leaving my arms and shoulders bare. Then I brushed back my hair and pulled it well down over my ears again. I put a lot of powder on my face so that the skin seemed even whiter than usual. I fished about until I found some old lip-salve, and I put oceans of it on my lips. Then I did under my eyes with burnt cork. Finally, I draped a red ribbon over my bare shoulder, stuck a scarlet feather in my hair, and placed a cigarette in one corner of my mouth. The whole effect pleased me very much.

'Anna the Adventuress,' I said aloud, nodding at my reflection. 'Anna the Adventuress, Episode I, "The House in Kensington!"

Girls are foolish things.

From *The Man in the Brown Suit*, 1924 | Agatha Christie (1890–1976)

When I open the doors of my cramped wardrobe with its jammed rails, the clear plastic bags containing cashmere sweaters sheltering against the predatory attentions of moths, the handbags in their own cotton bags, the folded jeans, the rows of colours (Black, purples, greens, browns, navy, white), the coats, the dresses, the jackets, the tops, I see a frozen frame. Me, spring 2008. This is the size I am. This is what I own.

There are nostalgic items I do not wear but do not want to throw away, and there are things that don't fit, and things that don't suit me, and things that were always a mistake, and things I mean to wear but don't, and the workhorses of my collection such as this Vanessa Bruno dress and that Anya Hindmarch cream handbag.

Out of the items in the wardrobe I will select the items that make up the self I plan to be that day.

But in the wardrobe there are also ghosts, absences, gaps and memories. The clothes I have owned have been an intimate and significant portion of my life. I have been another person when I wore them.

From *The Thoughtful Dresser: The Art of Adornment, the Pleasures of Shopping, and Why Clothes Matter*, 2009 | Linda Grant (b.1951)

To wash one's hair, make one's toilet, and put on sacred robes; even if not a soul sees one, these preparations still produce an inner pleasure.

From *The Pillow Book*, c.1000 AD | Sei Shōnagon (c.966–1017/1025 AD)

Chapter 6

FALLING IN LOVE

FALLING IN LOVE

Be Kind To Me

Gongyla, I ask only
that you wear the cream
white dress when you come

Desire darts about your
loveliness, drawn down in
circling flight at sight of it

and I am glad, although
once I too quarrelled
with Aphrodite
to whom
I pray that you will
come soon

Sappho (c.610–c.570 BC)

When modern women discovered the orgasm it was, combined with modern birth control, perhaps the biggest single nail in the coffin of male dominance.

Eva Figes (1932–2012)

She shines in the grocers shop in Sevenoaks with a candle lit radiance, stalking on legs like beech trees, pink glowing, grape clustered, pearl hung. That is the secret of her glamour, I suppose... There is her maturity & full breastedness: her being so much in full sail on the high tides... her being in short (what I have never been) a real woman.

Diary entry, 21 December 1925 | Virginia Woolf (1882–1941) on Vita Sackville-West

...I am reduced to a thing that wants Virginia. I composed a beautiful letter to you in the sleepless nightmare hours of the night, and it has all gone: I just miss you, in a quite simple desperate human way. You, with all your undumb letters, would never write so elementary a phrase as that; perhaps you wouldn't even feel it. And yet I believe you'll be sensible of a little gap. But you'd clothe it in so exquisite a phrase that it would lose a little of its reality. Whereas with me it is quite stark: I miss you even more than I could have believed; and I was prepared to miss you a good deal. So this letter is just really a squeal of pain. It is incredible how essential to me you have become. I suppose you are accustomed to people saying these things. Damn you, spoilt creature; I shan't make you love me any the more by giving myself away like this – but oh my dear, I can't be clever and stand-offish with you: I love you too much for that. Too truly. You have no idea how stand-offish I can be with people I don't love. I have brought it to a fine art. But you have broken down my defences. And I don't really resent it.

Vita Sackville-West (1892–1962) to Virginia Woolf, 21 January 1927

Sunday
52 Tavistock Square
Dearest Creature,
It was a very very nice letter you wrote by the light of the stars at midnight. Always write then, for your heart requires moonlight to deliquesce it. And mine is fried in gaslight, as it is only nine o'clock and I must go to bed at eleven. And so I shant say anything: not a word of the balm to my anguish – for I am always anguished – that you were to me. How I watched you! How I felt – now what was it like? Well, somewhere I have seen a little ball kept bubbling up and down on the spray of a fountain: the fountain is you, the ball me. It is a sensation I get only from you. It is physically stimulating, restful at the same time.

Virginia Woolf (1882–1941) to Vita Sackville-West, 7 October 1928

I'm alone. It is very cold and wet. I have got Virginia coming for the weekend. … Oh Hadji, she is such an angel; I really adore her. Not 'in love' but just love – devotion. I don't know whether it annoys you that I should write so often about her? One has to be so careful at this distance; but really Hadji shouldn't be annoyed, because her friendship does enrich me so, and she is so completely un-silly. I absolutely long for you to know her better. I don't think I have ever loved anybody so much, in the way of friendship; in fact, of course I haven't. She knows the mars adore each other; I've told her so, and so has Tray. [The mars were Vita and Harold, 'Hadji'.] Oh my sweet, they do, don't they? God, how I want to talk to you; just talk and talk and talk.

Vita Sackville-West (1892–1962) to Harold Nicolson, 30 November 1926

Women love too much; they allow love to over-ride everything else. Men don't. Or, rather, men see to it that the people who love them should submit themselves. I love you too much. You are much more important to me than anything else. That is the long and short of the matter...

But at least I do love you, incurably, ineradicably, and most oddly. That remains fixed. Immutable.

Vita Sackville-West (1892–1962) to Harold Nicolson, 13 December 1928

I Love You

I love your lips when they're wet with wine
And red with a wild desire;
I love your eyes when the lovelight lies
Lit with a passionate fire.
I love your arms when the warm white flesh
Touches mine in a fond embrace;
I love your hair when the strands enmesh
Your kisses against my face.

Not for me the cold, calm kiss
Of a virgin's bloodless love;
Not for me the saint's white bliss,
Nor the heart of a spotless dove.
But give me the love that so freely gives
And laughs at the whole world's blame,
With your body so young and warm in my arms,
It sets my poor heart aflame.

So kiss me sweet with your warm wet mouth,
Still fragrant with ruby wine,
And say with a fervor born of the South
That your body and soul are mine.
Clasp me close in your warm young arms,
While the pale stars shine above,
And we'll live our whole young lives away
In the joys of a living love.

Ella Wheeler Wilcox (1850–1919)

It was a peaceful, relaxed sort of party – I never felt one bit nervous, as I did when we went to dinner. (But the dinner-party was more thrilling; it glows in my memory like a dark picture with a luminous centre – candlelight and shining floors and the night pressing against the black windows.) Mrs Cotton was still away and Simon was very much the host, rather serious and just a bit stately, talking mainly to father and Topaz. Even with Rose he was surprisingly formal... she and I wandered around on our own and drifted into the biggest greenhouse. It was lovely moving through the hot, moist, heavily scented air and it felt particularly private – almost as if we were in a separate world from the others. Rose suddenly said:

'Oh, Cassandra, is it going to happen – is it?'

She looked as she used to on Christmas Eve, when we were hanging up our stockings.

'Are you really sure you want it to?' I asked – and then decided it was a wasted question when she was so obviously determined. To my surprise, she considered it a long time, staring out across the lawn to where Simon was talking with father and Topaz. A pink camellia fell with a little dead thud.

'Yes, quite sure,' she said at last, with an edge on her voice. 'Up to now, it's been like a tale I've been telling myself. Now it's real. And it's got to happen. It's got to.'

'Well, I feel as if it will,' I told her – and I really did. But greenhouses always give me a waiting, expectant sort of feeling.

From *I Capture the Castle*, 1949 | Dodie Smith (1896–1990)

My own Beloved, if ever you should have reason to complain of me in things voluntary and possible, all other women would have a right to tread me underfoot, I should be so vile and utterly unworthy. There is my answer to what you wrote yesterday of wishing to be better to me ... you! What could be better than lifting me from the ground and carrying me into life and the sunshine? I was yours rather by right than by gift (yet by gift also, my beloved!), for what you have saved and renewed is surely yours. All that I am I owe you – if I enjoy anything now and henceforth, it is through you.

Elizabeth Barrett Browning (1806–1861) to Robert Browning, 14 September 1846

Though I parted from you so lately, and though I expect to see you again so soon, yet I cannot keep my fingers from the pen but I must be plaguing you with my scrawl. Oh, my dearest love, I am never happy but when I am with you. I cannot speak or think of anything else. When shall we have another happy half hour?...

Let me see, what have I more to say? – nothing but the same dull story over and over again – that I love you to distraction, and that I would prefer you and beggary before any other man and a throne.

Elizabeth Linley (1754–1792) to R B Sheridan

'Twill be pleasinger to you, I am sure, to tell how fond I am of your lock. Well in earnest now, and setting aside all compliments, I never saw finer hair, nor of a better colour; but cut no more on't, I would not have it spoiled for the world. If you love me, be careful on't. I am combing, and curling, and kissing this lock all day, and dreaming on't all night.

Dorothy Osborne (1627–1695) to William Temple

You: an Achilles' apple
Blushing sweet on a high branch
At the tip of the tallest tree.
You escaped those who would pluck your fruit
Not that they didn't try. No,
They could not forget you
Poised beyond their reach.

Sappho (c.610–c.570BC), Fragment 105 (a)

Last night, there was a moment before you got into bed. You stood, quite naked, bending forward a little – talking. It was only for an instant. I saw you – I loved you so – loved your body with such tenderness – Ah my dear – And I am not thinking now of 'passion'. No, of that other thing that makes me feel that every inch of you is so precious to me. Your soft shoulders – your creamy warm skin, your ears, cold like shells are cold – your long legs and your feet that I love to clasp with my feet – the feeling of your belly – & your thin young back – Just below that bone that sticks out at the back of your neck you have a little mole. It is partly because we are so young that I feel this tenderness – I love your youth – I could not bear that should be touched even by a cold wind if I were the Lord. We two, you know have everything before us, and we shall do very great things – I have perfect faith in us – and so perfect is my love for you that I am, as it were, still, silent to my very soul. I want nobody but you for my lover and my friend and to nobody but you shall I be faithful.

I am yours for ever

Tig

Katherine Mansfield (1888–1923) to John Middleton Murry, 18 May, 1917

How shall I begin this letter? All the love names in the world are not enough. But you are to feel, as you read these lines, as though I held your head in my hands and were looking at you – a long, long look, before we kiss each other. It is absurd to say that I love you more. How could that be? And yet I do love you more. My precious one, love like ours hath no equal on this earth. I could not love you more; I always love you more.

Katherine Mansfield (1888–1923) to John Middleton Murry, 21 December 1917

If ever two were one, then surely we.
If ever man were lov'd by wife, then thee;
If ever wife was happy in a man,
Compare with me ye women if you can.
I prize thy love more than whole Mines of gold,
Or all the riches that the East doth hold.
My love is such that Rivers cannot quench,
Nor aught but love from thee, give recompense.
Thy love is such I can no way repay,
The heavens reward thee manifold I pray.

That while we live, in love lets so persevere,
That when we live no more, we may live ever.

Anne Bradstreet (1612–1672)

I look down the tracks and see you coming – and out of every haze and mist your darling rumpled trousers are hurrying to me – Without you, dearest dearest I couldn't see or hear or feel or think – or live – I love you so and I'm never in all our lives going to let us be apart another night. It's like begging for mercy of a storm of killing Beauty or growing old, without you. I want to kiss you so – and in the back where your dear hair starts and your chest – I love you – and I can't tell you how much...

Zelda Fitzgerald (1900–1948) to F Scott Fitzgerald, 1920

Yes, I did come to his bed with him, in that bedroom with its big open windows looking out over the nighttime and the quiet Balinese rice fields. He parted the sheer, white curtains of mosquito-netting that surrounded his bed and guided me in there. Then he helped me out of my dress with the tender competence of a man who had obviously spent many comfortable years getting his children ready for bathtime, and he explained to me his terms – that he wanted absolutely nothing from me whatsoever except permission to adore me for as long as I wanted him to. Were those terms acceptable to me?

Having lost my voice somewhere between the couch and the bed, I only nodded. There was nothing left to say. It had been a long, austere season of solitude. I had done well for myself. But Felipe was right – that was enough.

From *Eat, Pray, Love*, 2007 | Elizabeth Gilbert (b.1969)

My Lord,
My friend and I are now abed together a-contriving how to have your company this afternoon. If you deserve this favour, you will come and seek us at Ludgate Hill about three a clock at Butler's shop, where we will expect you, but lest we should give you too much satisfaction at once, we will say no more; expect the rest when you see us.
Your & c.

Anne Hamilton (1632–1716) and Barbara Villiers (1640–1709) to Lord Chesterfield, 1657

The sexual chemistry was what really surprised me, though. I thought he'd be one of those quiet types who was awkwardly gentle and clumsy, the sort of mild-mannered guy who says 'Am I hurting you?' when I can't feel a thing. But he was so attuned to my every movement I was sure he was reading my mind. He had no inhibitions, and whatever ones he discovered I had he'd pry away from me like little treasures. He saw all those private aspects of me - and I mean not just sexual private parts, but my darker side, my meanness, my pettiness, my self-loathing - all the things I kept hidden. So that with him I was completely naked, and when I was - when I was feeling the most vulnerable - when the wrong word would have sent me flying out the door forever - he always said exactly the right thing at the right moment. He didn't allow me to cover myself up. He would grab my hands, look me straight in the eye and tell me something new about why he loved me.

From *The Joy Luck Club*, 1989 | Amy Tan (b.1952)

I love men like some people like good food or wine.

From the *Observer*, 1979 | Germaine Greer (b.1939)

3 AM
Wide, wide, wide awake! I woke up thinking of Tracy [Chapman]. Remembering the curve of her leg when she's driving. The whiteness of her teeth when she smiles. The way she covers her face when she sleeps. The way I feel when she arrives & when she's driving away. How in the mornings I love to invite her into my arms.
My life is wonderful. Even witnessing all this pain [on a research trip to The Gambia] I am glad to be in life. Today I am 49, forty-nine...

Diary entry, 9 February 1993, from *Gathering Blossoms Under Fire*, 2022 | Alice Walker (b.1944)

Two last night. M– spoke in the very act. 'Ah,' said she, 'Can you ever love anyone else?' She knows how to heighten the pleasure of our intercourse. She often murmurs, 'Oh, how delicious,' just at the very moment. All her kisses are good ones...

Diary entry, 1824 | Anne Lister (1791–1840)

... There were a couple of spare wooden horses from the merry-go-round flaring their nostrils in one corner, and lots of smelly old sacks on the floor. We made them into a pile and sank down on them, the pungent dust rising around us. He kissed me for ages, much longer than my other boyfriends usually do, and soon I was longing for him to make love to me.

I knew, of course, that ultimately it would be disappointing – there would come a point when I would go dead and nothing would happen – so what happened next was a complete surprise.

He was inside me and kissing my breasts at the same time when I suddenly felt the most extraordinary sensation as if an electric current had been switched on, turning my whole body into a radiant powerhouse of sexual expectation. It was as though someone had mended a fuse in a dark room and all the lights had blazed on. For the first time I felt totally at home inside my own skin – not watching myself any longer from outside, I was really there, relaxed and letting go. My mind went dead, but my body was running away with me, and as our movements became faster and stronger it was like the long ride down from Flichity Inn, freewheeling all the way – look, no hands! – laughing and shouting with surprise and pleasure as I finally relaxed into joy.

Diary entry, 27 May 1945, from *Love is Blue: A Wartime Diary*, 1986 | Joan Wyndham (1921–2007)

In the weeks that followed we became more and more fond of each other, doing all the things that courting couples do without actually touching each other... Although we had not yet made love, I was completely happy and relaxed with him, with a feeling of expectancy, as if it was always Christmas morning. It was that thrilling period when two people know in their bones that something is going to happen, but want to prolong the waiting.

Then one night came the crunch. I went to have a bath and while I was out of the room Shura threw on a dressing-gown of black Chinese silk, lit six candles and an incense stick and laid out two glasses and a bottle of vodka on the ironing board. Then he seized the ukulele and flung himself on my bed. It was irresistible!

Diary entry, 1952, from *Anything Once*, 1993 | Joan Wyndham (1921–2007)

...At 1st, we thought someone [was] breaking into the house but the continuance of the noises & the pattering of rain soon ushered in a tremendous thunder storm. Very vivid, fast-succeeding flashes of lightning enlightened the whole room. After some time came 1 or 2 tremendous peals of thunder & the heaviest rain I almost ever heard. In the midst of all this, we drew close together, made love & had one of the most delightfully long, tender kisses we have ever had. Said she, in the midst of it, 'Oh, don't leave me yet.' This renewed and redoubled my feelings & we slept in each other's arms.

Diary entry, 14 September 1823 | Anne Lister (1791–1840)

We didn't say much more. Love is a wordless communion between two people. That night we went back to that little yellow house in Nichols Canyon and made love. And, oh, God, it was magic. We became lovers forever - eternally. Big words, I know. But I truly felt that no matter what happened we would always be in love. And God almighty, things did happen.

Frank [Sinatra] and I didn't hide ourselves away...

I didn't understand then and, frankly, I still don't understand now why there should be this prurient mass hysteria about a male and female climbing into bed and doing what comes naturally. It's blessed in weddings, celebrated in honeymoons, but out of wedlock it's condemned as the worst of sins. Maybe people are paying too much attention to the 'lock' part of wedlock. And maybe, just maybe, there's a touch of jealousy somewhere.

From *Ava: My Story*, 1990 | Ava Gardner (1922–1990)

Most women have a special sexual fantasy. Mine was to make love on a bed covered with gardenias. Once I was in love with a man famous in the music world... One day at the height of our romance, he reserved a suite at the Waldorf-Astoria in New York. To my delight and amazement, the bed was covered with gardenias. When the maids were tidying up the room next day, what did they think..?

From *This 'N' That*, 1982 | Bette Davis (1908–1989)

Tightly clutching her bag she sat through the news reel, all sport and soldiers, the comic, all American slang that she could not understand, and the big romance, which brought tears to her eyes. Lovely, she thought it. It filled her with vague longings.

She looked at the languishing lady on the screen and saw sinuous movements, hips slim as a whiting's, wet dark lips and lashes luxuriant as goose-grass in a hedge bottom. She thought: I'm a back number. Nobody wants me. The boys are sick of me. She remembered her square, uncompromising reflection in the polished mirror above her chest of drawers.

The star on the sofa leant back to receive her lover's passionate embrace.

Well now, that's not what I'd call nice, criticised Mrs. Brimsley. If I caught one of my girls carrying on like that, I know what I'd do to her.

Yet she had her memories.

From *South Riding*, 1936 | Winifred Holtby (1898–1935)

In the course of this working and vital summer, we have mystically become one. I can appreciate the legend of Eve coming from Adam's ribs I never did before; the damn story's true! That's where I belong.

Away from Ted, I feel as if I were living with one eyelash of myself only. It is really agony... My poems and stories I want to be the strongest female paean yet for the creative forces of nature, the joy of being a loved and loving woman; that is my song.

Sylvia Plath (1932–1963) to her mother, 8 October 1956

Being in love (*l'amour fou*) ['crazy love'] a pathological variant of loving. Being in love + addiction, obsession, exclusion of others, insatiable demand for presence, paralysis of other interests and activities. A disease of love, a fever (therefore exalting). One 'falls' in love. But this is one disease which, if one must have it, it is better to have often rather than infrequently. It's less mad to fall in love often (less inaccurate for there are many wonderful people in the world) than only two or three times in one's life. Or maybe it's better always to be in love with several people at any given time,

Diary entry, 15 February 1970, from *As Consciousness is Harnessed to Flesh*, 2012 | Susan Sontag (1933–2004)

Miss Hogmanimy would enlarge upon how alcohol leads to irregularity in sexual behaviour. Oh what a lovely phrase that is, and how it does not describe the way you feel at parties sometimes, if you have your right friends there, and that lovely feeling, you get quite shot up, and it is lovely oh how I enjoy it.

From *Novel on Yellow Paper, or, Work it out for yourself*, 1936 | Stevie Smith (1902–1971)

I didn't make any mistake. I know that when [Simon] nearly asked me to marry him it was only an impulse – just as it was when he kissed me on Midsummer Eve; a mixture of liking me very much and longing for Rose. It is part of a follow-my-leader game of second-best we have all been playing...

It isn't a bit of use pretending I'm not crying, because I am... Pause to mop up. Better now.

Perhaps it would really be rather dull to be married and settled for life. Liar! It would be heaven.

Only half a page left now. Shall I fill it up with 'I love you, I love you' – like father's page of cats on the mat. No. Even a broken heart doesn't warrant a waste of good paper.

There is a light down in the castle kitchen. Tonight I shall have my bath in front of the fire, with Simon's gramophone playing. Topaz has it on now, much too loud – to bring father back to earth in time for tea – but it sounds beautiful from this distance. She is playing the Berceuse from Stravinsky's 'The Firebird'. It seems to say: 'What shall I do? Where shall I go?'

You will go in to tea, my girl – and a much better tea than you would have come by this time last year.

A mist is rolling over the fields. Why is summer mist romantic and autumn mist just sad?

There was mist on Midsummer Eve, mist when we drove into the dawn.

He said he would come back.

Only the margin left to write on now. I love you, I love you, I love you.

From *I Capture the Castle*, 1949 | Dodie Smith (1896–1990)

Late in the night he tells me about a book I have not read, Arthur Machen's Hill of Dreams. And I am listening with my soul. He says softly, 'I'm talking almost paternally to you.'

At that moment I know I am half woman, half child. That a portion of me conceals a child who loves to be amazed, to be taught, to be directed. When I listen, I am a child, and Henry becomes paternal. The haunting image of an erudite, literary father reasserts itself, and the woman becomes small again. I remember other phrases, like 'I would not hurt you – not you,' his unusual delicacy with me, his protectiveness. I feel myself betrayed. Overwhelmed by the wonder of Henry's work, I have become a child. I can imagine another man saying to me, 'I cannot make love to you. You are not a woman. You are a child.'

I awake from dreams of utter sensuality. And then in anger I want to dominate, to work like a man, support Henry, get his book published. I want more than ever to fuck and be fucked, to assert the sensual woman. Henry says one day, 'Listen, I believe you could have ten lovers and handle them all. You're insatiable.' And another day, 'Your sensuality doesn't convince me.'

He has seen the child!

Hateful, infuriating. I run away from Clichy and think I carry my secret away with me. I have the hope that Henry has not grasped it too well. I fear the uncanny analysis of his eyes. I slip out of his bed and run away while he sleeps. I rush home and fall asleep, deeply, for many hours. I must choke the child. Tomorrow I can meet Henry, face him, be woman.

From *Henry and June*, 1986 | Anaïs Nin (1903–1977)

Most of the younger women and some of the older ones were fond of what they called 'a bit of a read', and their mental fare consisted almost exclusively of the novelette. Several of the hamlet women took in one of these weekly, as published, for the price was but one penny, and these were handed round until the pages were thin and frayed with use. Copies of others found their way there from neighbouring villages, or from daughters in service, and there was always quite a library of them in circulation.

The novelette of the 'eighties was a romantic love story, in which the poor governess always married the duke, or the lady of title the gamekeeper, who always turned out to be a duke or an earl in disguise. Midway through the story there had to be a description of a ball, at which the heroine in her simple white gown attracted all the men in the room...

From *Lark Rise to Candleford*, 1945 | Flora Thompson (1876–1947)

To meet one's lover summer is indeed the right season. True, the nights are very short, and dawn creeps up before one has had a wink of sleep. Since all the lattices have been left open, one can lie and look out at the garden in the cool morning air. There are still a few endearments to exchange before the man takes his leave, and the lovers are murmuring to each other when suddenly there is a loud noise. For a moment they are certain that they have been discovered, but it is only the caw of a crow flying past in the garden.

An attractive woman, whose hair tumbles loosely over her forehead, has received a letter in the dark. Evidently she is too impatient to wait for a lamp; instead she takes some fire-tongs, and, lifting a piece of burning charcoal from the brazier, laboriously reads by its pale light. It is a charming scene.

From *The Pillow Book*, c.1000AD | Sei Shōnagon (c.966–1017/1025 AD)

16 September 1890
Tio got up even later than usual this morning; he simply can't leave me and often returns about 11 o'clock so that we can have caresses that never end.

18 September 1890
Tio was perfectly mad tonight – he kissed me passionately even in front of Amalia and Bertie, which ended in the most delicious love making. He really is a stallion – 4 times.

28 November 1890
Delirium. Afterwards Tio said, 'Was it nice, Vicky?'

27 June 1891, Knole
What a heavenly husband I have and how different our love and union is from that of other couples.

Diary entries, 1890–1891 | Lady Sackville (1892–1936)

Osia, my beloved, faraway sweetheart!

I have no words, my darling, to write this letter that you may never read, perhaps. I am writing it into empty space. Perhaps you will come back and not find me here. Then this will be all you have left to remember me by.

Osia, what a joy it was living together like children – all our squabbles and arguments, the games we played, and our love. Now I do not even look at the sky. If I see a cloud, who can I show it to?...

My every thought is about you. My every tear and every smile is for you. I bless every day and every hour of our bitter life together, my sweetheart, my companion, my blind guide in life.

Like two blind puppies we were, nuzzling each other and feeling so good together. And how fevered your poor head was, and how madly we frittered away the days of our life. What joy it was, and how we always knew what joy it was.

From *Hope Abandoned*, a letter to her husband, the poet Osip Mandelstam, who had just been taken away by Stalin's secret police | Nadezhda Mandelstam (1899–1980), translated by Max Hayward, 1974

My darling,

It was a real event in my life and my heart to be with you the other day. We do matter to each other, don't we? however much our ways may have diverged. I think we have got something indestructible between us, haven't we? Even right back to the library seat in your papa's room at Grosvenor Street - and then at Duntreath - and then to everything that came afterwards. Glissons, mortels... but what a bond, Lushka darling; a bond of childhood and subsequent passion, such as neither of us will ever share with anyone else.

It has been a very strange relationship, ours; unhappy at times, happy at others; but unique in its way, but infinitely precious to me and (may I say?) to you.

What I like about it is that we always come together again however long the gaps in our meetings may have been. Time seems to make no difference. This is a sort of love letter I suppose. Odd that I should be writing you a love letter after all these years - when we have written so many to each other. Parce que c'était lui, parce que c'était moi.

Oh, you sent me a book about Elizabeth Barrett Browning. Thank you, darling generous Lushka and you gave me a coal-black briquet. It lights up into the flame of love which always burns in my heart whenever I think of you. You said it would last for three months, but our love has lasted for forty years and more. Your Mitya

Vita Sackville-West (1892–1962) to Violet Trefusis, 3 September 1950

But this question of love (she thought, putting her coat away), this falling in love with women. Take Sally Seton; her relation in the old days with Sally Seton. Had not that, after all, been love?

...The strange thing, on looking back, was the purity, the integrity, of her feeling for Sally. It was not like one's feeling for a man. It was completely disinterested, and besides, it had a quality which could only exist between women, between women just grown up. It was protective, on her side: sprang from a sense of being in league together, a presentiment of something that was bound to part them (they spoke of marriage always as a catastrophe), which led to this chivalry, this protective feeling which was much more on her side than Sally's. For in those days she was completely reckless; did the most idiotic things out of bravado; bicycled round the parapet on the terrace: smoked cigars. Absurd, she was – very absurd. But the charm was overpowering, to her at least, so that she could remember standing in her bedroom at the top of the house holding the hot-water can in her hands and saying aloud, 'She is beneath this roof... She is beneath this roof!'

From *Mrs Dalloway*, 1925 | Virginia Woolf (1882–1941)

... I doubt if any man's love equals a woman's love for a woman when it is healthy and genuine. Would any man have cared for Miss Heath-Jones as my aunt has done? Will Gordon ever be so good to me as you are? I doubt it. Fond as I am of him, I shall never, I think, have the same complete, unshadowed reliance on his benevolence as I have on yours. With men there is always a little *arrière-pensée* of their own comfort, their own convenience. So there is with many women (including myself), but I have never found it in you as regards me, or in my aunt as regards Miss Heath-Jones.

Dear, dear sweetieheart. More than I can say I long to get back to you. I suppose my longing is wholly selfish, but it isn't a longing which wants to spoil anything you are doing, only to have the stimulus of your presence. You warm me like a beautiful summer day.

Ever, my darling one, your v.s.v.d.l.

Vera Brittain (1893–1970) to Winifred Holtby, 15 May 1927

The journey would have been pleasant in most circumstances, and interesting in any, but because you were there it was wholly delightful. Whatever things may happen in the future of good or evil, at least we have had one perfect time which nothing can take away...

Our actions all have immortality;
Such gladness gives no hostage unto death.

Thank you, thank you, thank you, for being so completely satisfactory, you most sweet woman. And we will go again. There are heaps of lovely places to see, and things to do. Never doubt I want to see them and do them, and that I ask no better travelling companion than you.

Winifred Holtby (1898–1935) to Vera Brittain following a shared trip to Italy, 19 October 1921

I love you in a way that part of me has become part of you. When you are troubled, so must I be, whether I like it or not. When you are happy, part of me is happy, whatever else befalls. Only be happy, my sweet. Fulfil yourself, as you must with joys and pains and enriched experience. I who am part of you, can only gain by your gains. This you must and shall believe. I do not want a shadow of doubt to cross your mind about this – for it would be a false doubt.

For myself, I have one of my own peculiar little private joys today – flowers in profusion, a lime tree outside my window, a broad, clear table, and a ream of new paper.

Darling sweet, I love you. I also think that your husband is very nice. Give him my love. Of course he may read any of my letters that interest him sufficiently.

My sweet my pretty, I kiss your clear head. W.

Winifred Holtby (1898–1935) to Vera Brittain, 29 July 1925

It is strange to see how impassioned this love is, how many tears, penances and prayers it costs; how careful is the loving soul to commend the object of its affection to all who it thinks may prevail with God and ask them to intercede with Him for it; and how constant is its longing, so that it cannot be happy unless it sees that its loved one is making progress. If that soul seems to have advanced, and is then seen to fall some way back, her friend seems to have no more pleasure in life: she neither eats than sleeps, is never free from this fear and is always afraid that the soul whom she loves so much may be lost, and that the two may be parted for ever.

From *The Way of Perfection*, 1583 | St Teresa of Avila (1515–1582)

August 26, 1997
It has been a most extraordinary week. Zelie is wonderful. Warm, loving, spontaneous, fun. And a delicious lover! She introduced me to the most intense, fun sex I've ever experienced. I never knew it was possible to laugh so much or to orgasm with such joy. And we also talk & walk & travel & eat together well. And swim & cook.

We love being together. Sleeping together. She is so natural. The most natural person – next to my daddy! – I've met. And she too has aches & pains, which I try to soothe. I love this – I get to take care of her.

Diary entry, 26 August 1997, from *Gathering Blossoms Under Fire*, 2022 | Alice Walker (b.1944)

I'm so afraid you'll forget me dear Emily – through these cold winter days, when I cannot come to see you, that I cannot forbear writing the least little bit of a note – to put you in mind of me; perhaps it will make you laugh – it may be foolish in me but I love you so well sometimes – not that I do not always – but more dearly sometimes – and with such desire to see you that I find myself addressing you almost ere I'm aware. When I am as old as you and have had so many friends, perhaps they wont seem so precious, and then I shant write any more little 'billet doux' like these, but you will forgive me now, because I cant find so many dear to me as you...

Emily Dickinson (1830–1886) to Emily Fowler (Ford)

I promised you my Dearest Dearest Love, a plan, of my ideas for your future life – here it is, but remember, that one word of yours as to any other intention will be adopted by me, unless indeed they were such as would hurt your health or deprive me of the happiness of seeing you.

The summit of my wishes would be that whilst you remain abroad you would not only attend strictly to your dear health, but likewise to every amusement for your mind that would not be hurtful to it or imprudent... When you do return it will be to Devonshire House, for a month at least... I will look out immediately for a house for you near us, on condition you are less in it than here.

Georgiana, Duchess of Devonshire (1757–1806) to Bess Foster, February 1783

Who has any right to know how long or how tenderly we love one another! Why are excuses to be made for its sharpness and its fervency? Why am I to pay court to anybody but your mother? Why is our union to be profaned by having a lie told about it? Can I ever forget the note that contains – 'the first instant I saw you, my heart flew to your service'... Does the warm impulse of two hearts want an excuse to be accounted for, and must your partiality to me be ushered in by another connection?

Bess Foster (1758–1824), *later Georgiana's successor as Duchess of Devonshire*, to Georgiana, 17 January 1784

...whenever a single woman over forty brings up the topic of love, again and again the assumption, rooted in sexist thinking, is that she is 'desperate' for a man. No one thinks she is simply passionately intellectually interested in the subject matter. No one thinks she is rigorously engaged in a philosophical undertaking wherein she is endeavouring to understand the metaphysical meaning of love...

From *All About Love*, 2000 | bell hooks (1952–2021)

Self preservation is the first law of nature, are married women then the only part of human nature that must not follow it? [Women have] superior sense, superior fortitude and reason [to men]... how dangerous is Power in women's hands? Do I know so many miserable wives from man's tyrannical power... His honour is now mine: had I none before I married? Can I divide them? how lose his, and keep my own?

Henrietta Howard, Countess of Suffolk (1689–1767) on seeking a separation from her abusive husband, 29 August 1716

It's not till sex has died out between a man and a woman that they can really love. And now I mean affection. Now I mean to be fond of (as one is fond of oneself) – to hope, to be disappointed, to live inside the other heart. When I look back on the pain of sex, the love like a wild fox so ready to bite, the antagonism that sits like a twin beside love, and contrast it with affection, so deeply unrepeatable, of two people who have lived a life together (and of whom one must die), it's the affection I find richer. It's that I would have again. Not all those doubtful rainbow colours (but then she's old, one must say).

From *Autobiography*, 1969 | Enid Bagnold (1889–1991)

As her husband advanced up the path she had a sudden vision of their three years together. Those years were her whole life; everything before them had been colorless and unconscious, like the blind life of the plant before it reaches the surface of the soil. The years had not been exactly what she had dreamed; but if they had taken away certain illusions they had left richer realities in their stead. She understood now that she had gradually adjusted herself to the new image of her husband as he was, as he would always be. He was not the hero of her dreams, but he was the man she loved, and who had loved her. For she saw now, in this last wide flash of pity and initiation, that, as a comely marble may be made out of worthless scraps of mortar, glass and pebbles, so out of mean mixed substances may be fashioned a love that will bear the stress of life.

From *Tales of Men and Ghosts*, 1910 | Edith Wharton (1862–1937)

Marriage, which has been the bourne of so many narratives, is still a great beginning, as it was to Adam and Eve, who kept their honeymoon in Eden, but had their first little one among the thorns and thistles of the wilderness. It is still the beginning of the home epic – the gradual conquest or irredeemable loss of that complete union which makes the advancing years a climax, and age the harvest of sweet memories in common.

Some set out, like the Crusaders of old, with a glorious equipment of hope and enthusiasm and get broken by the way, wanting patience with each other and the world.

All who have cared for Fred Vincy and Mary Garth will like to know that these two made no such failure, but achieved a solid mutual happiness...

On inquiry it might possibly be found that Fred and Mary still inhabit Stone Court – that the creeping plants still cast the foam of their blossoms over the fine stonewall into the field where the walnut-trees stand in stately row – and that on sunny days the two lovers who were first engaged with the umbrella-ring may be seen in white-haired placidity at the open window from which Mary Garth, in the days of old Peter Featherstone, had often been ordered to look out for Mr Lydgate.

From *Middlemarch*, 1871 | George Eliot (1819–1880)

I suppose one of the strangest things about my trio of failed marriages... was the fact that the marriage bond seemed to be a shackle that manacled us together. Once divorced, we enjoyed each other and retained a deep friendship. And more than anyone else, that was true between Frank [Sinatra] and me...

We might have been in different cities, different countries, but we were never apart. And every once in a while, Frank would call me in Madrid, London, Rome, New York, wherever I happened to be, and say, 'Ava, let's try again.' And I'd say, 'Okay!' and drop everything, sometimes even a part in a picture. And it would be heaven, but it wouldn't last more than twenty-four hours. And I'd go running off again, literally running. We could never quite understand why it hadn't and couldn't work out.

From *Ava: My Story*, 1990 | Ava Gardner (1922–1990)

Dearest,
I feel certain that I am going mad again... So I am doing what seems the best thing to do. You have given me the greatest possible happiness. You have been in every way all that anyone could be. I don't think two people could have been happier until this terrible disease came... I owe all the happiness of my life to you. You have been utterly patient with me and incredibly good. I want to say that – everybody knows it. If anybody could have saved me it would have been you.

Virginia Woolf (1882–1941), her last letter to her husband Leonard, 28 March 1941

So it slowly dawned on me on the airplane out of Dallas – my world now turned back-to-front, my lover exiled, the two of us having effectively been sentenced to marry – that perhaps I should use this time to somehow make peace with the idea of matrimony before I jumped into it once again. Perhaps it would be wise to put a little effort into unravelling the mystery of what in the name of God and human history this befuddling, vexing, contradictory, and yet stubbornly enduring institution of marriage actually is.

From *Committed*, 2010 | Elizabeth Gilbert (b.1969)

Friendship After Love

After the fierce midsummer all ablaze
  Has burned itself to ashes, and expires
  In the intensity of its own fires,
There come the mellow, mild, St. Martin days
Crowned with the calm of peace, but sad with haze.
  So after Love has led us, till he tires
  Of his own throes, and torments, and desires,
Comes large-eyed friendship: with a restful gaze,
He beckons us to follow, and across
  Cool verdant vales we wander free from care.
  Is it a touch of frost lies in the air?
Why are we haunted with a sense of loss?
We do not wish the pain back, or the heat;
And yet, and yet, these days are incomplete.

Ella Wheeler Wilcox (1850–1919)

At some point, everyone has to lose the one they feel they can't live without. Within all my anger, sorrow and grief, there was also this idea that the video game of life had taken an interesting turn. I didn't ever intend to end up here, so that became the question: 'How might I not only survive this, but might this be the doorway to a life I'd never asked for?'. Just as there was life I could only have with Rayya, there was a life I could only have without her. ... When I'm in love with somebody, I give them everything and do everything for them. I thought, 'What if I treated myself with that same level of devotion, rather than constantly looking to the other person? What is my joy?'

From BODY+SOUL, 16 January 2025 | Elizabeth Gilbert (b.1969)

Alfred and I are happy, as happy as married people can be. We are in love, we are intellectually and physically suited in every possible way, we rejoice in each other's company. We have no money troubles and three delightful children. And yet when I consider my life, day by day, hour by hour, it seems to be composed of a series of pinpricks... These are the components of marriage, the wholemeal bread of life, rough, ordinary but sustaining.

From *The Pursuit of Love*, 1945 | Nancy Mitford (1904–1973)

Autumn

He told his life story to Mrs Courtly
Who was a widow. 'Let's get married shortly',
He said. 'I am no longer passionate,
But we can have some conversation before it is too late.'

Stevie Smith (1902–1971)

Chapter 7

FOUNDATIONS

FOUNDATIONS

A woman's best protection is a little money of her own.

Clare Boothe Luce (1903–1987)

It is necessary to have five hundred a year and a room with a lock on the door to write fiction or poetry.

From *A Room of One's Own*, 1929 | Virginia Woolf (1882–1941)

From ***The Land***

She walks among the loveliness she made
Between the apple-blossom and the water –
She walks among the patterned pied brocade
Each flower her son, and every tree her daughter.

From 'The Land', 1926 | Vita Sackville-West (1892–1962)

But what truly horsey girls discover in the end is that boyfriends, husbands, children and careers are the substitute – for horses.

Jane Smiley (b.1949)

If there's one thing in my life that I am proud of, it's that I've never been a kept woman.

Marilyn Monroe (1926–1962)

My aunt, Mary Beton, I must tell you, died by a fall from her horse when she was riding out to take the air in Bombay. The news of my legacy reached me one night about the same time that the act was passed that gave votes to women. A solicitor's letter fell into the post-box and when I opened it I found that she had left me five hundred pounds a year for ever. Of the two – the vote and the money – the money, I own, seemed infinitely the most important...

...No force in the world can take from me my five hundred pounds. Food, house and clothing are mine forever. Therefore not merely do effort and labour cease, but also hatred and bitterness. I need not hate any man; he cannot hurt me. I need not flatter any man; he has nothing to give me. So imperceptibly I found myself adopting a new attitude towards the other half of the human race.

From *A Room of One's Own*, 1929 | Virginia Woolf (1882–1941)

This is not a story about a woman who made the best of traditional skills. This is a story about a woman who did her own IPO. This is the 'woman's pluck' story, the dust-bowl story, the burying-your-child-on-the-trail story, the I-will-never-go-hungry-again story, the Mildred Pierce story, the story about how the sheer nerve of even professionally unskilled women can prevail, show the men; the story that has historically encouraged women in this country, even as it has threatened men. The dreams and fears into which Martha Stewart taps are not of 'feminine' domesticity but of female power, of the woman who sits down at the table with the men and, still in her apron, walks away with the chips.

From *Let Me Tell You What I Mean*, 2021 | Joan Didion (1934–2021) on Martha Stewart

I truly believe that women should be financially independent from their men. And let's face it, money gives men the power to run the show. It gives men the power to define value. They define what's sexy. And men define what's feminine. It's ridiculous.

Beyoncé (b.1981)

I imagine that a few of the gentlefolks of Cranford were poor, and had some difficulty in making both ends meet; but they were like the Spartans, and concealed their smart under a smiling face. We none of us spoke of money, because that subject savoured of commerce and trade, and though some might be poor, we were all aristocratic. The Cranfordians had that kindly esprit de corps which made them overlook all deficiencies in success when some among them tried to conceal their poverty. ... It was considered 'vulgar' (a tremendous word in Cranford) to give anything expensive, in the way of eatable or drinkable, at the evening entertainments. Wafer bread-and-butter and sponge-biscuits were all that the Honourable Mrs Jamieson gave; and she was sister-in-law to the late Earl of Glenmire, although she did practise such 'elegant economy.'

'Elegant economy!' How naturally one falls back into the phraseology of Cranford! There, economy was always 'elegant' and money-spending always 'vulgar and ostentatious'; a sort of sour-grapism which made us very peaceful and satisfied.

From *Cranford*, 1853 | Mrs Gaskell (1810–1865)

Women with money and women with power are two uncomfortable ideas in our society.

Candace Bushnell (b.1958)

The education bestowed on Flora Poste by her parents had been expensive, athletic and prolonged, and when they died within a few weeks of one another during the annual epidemic of influenza or Spanish Plague which occurred in her twentieth year she was discovered to possess every art and grace save that of earning her own living.

From *Cold Comfort Farm*, 1932 | Stella Gibbons (1902–1989)

Worshipful cousin, I commend me to you, desiring to hear of your health and heart's ease, which I beseech God send you. And as for my little cousin, your son is a fair child and a merry, blessed be to God.

Cousin, the cause of my writing at this time is for certain evidences of Frethorp that I delivered my cousin your husband for to have made award betwixt Rammesbury and me, and 1 book of paper of the customs of Ormesby and 1 roll called 'domesday' and certain other evidences belonging to the said manor... Wherefore, cousin, I beseech you heartily that when you look among your evidences that you will lay them apart for me, as my very trust is that you will, for I hear say that you have right well and conscientiously delivered certain persons the evidence belonging to them and I trust verily you will the same to me.

Elizabeth Clere to Margaret Paston (c.1466)

I have always had a great relationship with money, even when I barely had any to relate to. I never fear not having it and never obsessed about what I had.

Oprah Winfrey (b.1954)

Life is to be lived. If you have to support yourself, you had bloody well better find some way that is going to be interesting. And you don't do that by sitting around wondering about yourself.

Katherine Hepburn (1907–2003)

I must say I hate money, but it's the lack of it that I hate most.

Katherine Mansfield (1888–1923)

...'Money', said Mlle [Coco] Chanel suddenly, 'is the ladder to success. When it comes in plenty, you cease to think much about it, and yet beware! You must not neglect it, for its management requires great skill. Knowing how to look after money is correlative to success in business.

'When I interview a prospective mannequin, I say to her: "Do you want to do this more than anything else? Or do you merely see it as a convenient way of wearing nice clothes and being smartly turned out? If it is just a question of wanting to have your hair dressed by Carita or Guillaume, and learning how to make yourself up, you will never be anything more than a pretty girl. You need to be madly in love with your job".'

From *The Dream Makers*, 1961 | Mrs Robert Henrey (1906–2004)

O gad I am so sick of bills for my part, I believe I shall never be able to hear 'em mention'd without casting up my accounts *vomiting*. I have paid one this morning as Long as my arme & as broad as my bum.

Mary Bellenden (1685–1736), *court beauty*, to Henrietta Howard, c.1716

One must have a home, you see, to keep one's books in and one's spring sofas; but the charm of a home is it is a home to come back to.

Elizabeth Barrett Browning (1806–1861) to Mary Russell Mitford, 13 November 1850

If I am to write, I must have a room to myself, which shall be my room. I have in my own mind pitched on Mrs. Whipple's room. We can put a stove in it. I have bought a cheap carpet for it, and there is furniture enough at home to furnish it comfortably, and I only beg in addition that you will let me change the glass door from the nursery into that room and keep my plants there, and then I shall be quite happy.

All last winter I felt the need of some place where I could go and be quiet and satisfied. I could not there, for there was all the setting of tables, and clearing up of tables, and dressing and washing of children, and everything else going on, and the continual falling of soot and coal dust on everything was a constant annoyance to me, and I never felt comfortable there, though I tried hard. Then if I came into the parlor where you were, I felt as if I were interrupting you, and I know you sometimes thought so, too.

Harriet Beecher Stowe (1811–1896) to her husband, 1841

My fascination with owning houses, which is in a way against my nature – I don't innately like owning things – comes from the desire to make where I live beautiful, comfortable; a place where everything works.

In Mexico because my Spanish is minor and because I'm here only once a year, and because there's so much culturally & politically I don't understand, it is impossible – or seems so – for things to work as smoothly as I might wish. (The whole country doesn't work!) Not that ours does.

And yet, when I'm here alone I focus on the good, the beautiful. Yet when others are here I seem to see only the faults. I tend to see my little house through their eyes and to judge it harshly. In fact, I abandon it, and this abandonment makes me feel divided, disloyal and sad.

I feared the arrival of my friends Joan & Sue! Would they like what they found? Would the four of us be happy? They arrived laughing and whole. Admiring of everything. Sue especially is so appreciative. The flowers, the trees, the birds, the air! She lifted my heart. Joan as well. Soon I was – the nine year old – seeing my little 'shack' through the eyes of love. And yes! I said. Isn't this wonderful! And that too. And come let me show you something else! I was incredibly happy that they were happy.

**Diary entry, 9 January 1998, from *Gathering Blossoms Under Fire*, 2022 |
Alice Walker (b.1944)**

With Chéri out of the house, Léa became once again lighter, lively, very much awake. In less than an hour, she had been bathed, rubbed down with spirit scented with sandal-wood, hatted, and shod. While the curling-tongs heated up, she found time to skim the maître d'hôtel's account book, to send for Émile, the footman, and point out the blue haze on a mirror. She cast an experienced eye – almost never taken in – over everything in the room, and dined in solitary bliss, smiling at the dry Vouvray and the June strawberries, served with their stalks on a Rubelles platter, green as a tree-frog after rain.

From *Chéri*, 1920 | Colette (1873–1954)

...If I could, I'd gather my dear, wide-windowed house and take it far away, *from the bombing*, and hide it safely in some quiet spot. I lived so long in a dark old house where, try as I would, sun and air did not linger. It's not a good attitude of mind, I know – 'Thou shalt not make any graven image' – and after all, it's only a semi-jerry-built modern house, with little of value in it. I keep telling myself that, but then the soft sheen of my 'autumn-tiled' fireplace or my gay bright curtain, or the polished, panelled hall takes my eye... and my hand goes to stroke a cushion or curtain, or to move my brass tray to catch the sun.

Diary entry, 14 March 1941, from *Nella Last's War* | Nella Last (1889–1968)

My friend Gemma said to me, 'You have to get your bedroom working for you. Build a desk. Build shelves. Bring up the boxes from the garage and unpack your books. Have a go at living with colour.' By this she meant painting the walls a colour that was not white. 'Yellow would be good for you,' she insisted. 'It clears up emotions and gives us a bigger sense of things.' When she said that, I remembered painting the bedroom ceiling in the family house with a colour called English Skylight. The ceiling looked like a dull leaden sky. Even when the sun was shining outside, it was raining inside. Every day and every night.

In my new life I was going to commit to living with colour.

I painted the walls in my bedroom yellow. I bought sumptuous orange silk curtains in a charity shop. I put up an African shield made from chicken feathers that had been dyed pink. It was two foot wide and looked like a large full-blown flower. The shield was stitched together in a way that allowed it to open and close. Yet nailed to the wall it was always open at a time when I was emotionally closed. I needed a shield to defend myself from the rage of my old life. I suppose I could say that I was now shielded by a flower.

From *The Cost of Living*, 2018 | Deborah Levy (b.1959)

Well. Then we had the irises, rising beautiful and cool on their tall stalks, like blown glass, like crystal water momentarily frozen in a splash, light blue, light mauve, and the darker ones, velvet and purple, black cat's ears in the sun, indigo shadow, and the bleeding hearts, so female in shape it was a surprise they'd not long since been rooted out. There is something subversive about this garden of Serena's, a sense of buried things bursting upwards, wordlessly, into the light, as if to point, to say: Whatever is silenced will clamour to be heard, though silently.

From *The Handmaid's Tale*, 1985 | Margaret Atwood (b.1939)

It was zero this morning. I have a fire burning in my study, yellow roses and mimosa on my desk. There is an atmosphere of festival, of release, in the house. We are one, the house and I, and I am happy to be alone – time to think, time to be. This kind of open-ended time is the only luxury that really counts and I feel stupendously rich to have it. And for the moment I have a sense of fulfillment both about my life and about my work that I have rarely experienced until this year, or perhaps until these last weeks. I look to my left and the transparent blue sky behind a flame-colored cyclamen, lifting about thirty winged flowers to the light, makes an impression of stained-glass, light-flooded.

Diary entry, 8 January 1971, from *Journal of a Solitude*, 1973 | May Sarton (1912–1995)

I had never been on a proper cruise ship, so there had been anxieties. Would I be troubled by someone's attempt to decorate the cabin into a similitude of a floating hotel? ...I braced myself for disappointment as I opened the door, but found instead nine foot by seven and a half foot of wish-fulfilment.

Cabin 532 was quite as right as it could be, and in recognition of this I let out a gasp and then laughed at the improbability of my being here, far from anywhere and entirely, at that moment, satisfied with my environment. Plain white walls, a desk, a book shelf above it, cupboards ranged along one wall with a small built-in fridge... The bedding, to my delight, was all white. Sheet, pillow cases and thin padded duvet, neatly folded and ship-shape. White, all-white. Opposite the door was a large rectangular window - porthole if you must - which opened wide. Nothing else. It was a monk's cell. Not the medieval version which I knew would be too physically rigorous for my gratification-seeking soma, but a modern version, for a latter-day monk spoiled by central heating and the pleasures of square feather pillows, with an effete belief that the workings of the mind are enhanced by the comfort of the body.

From *Skating to Antarctica*, 1997 | Jenny Diski (1947–2016)

A bright fire burnt in the grate, and some palest orchid-mauve silk curtains were drawn in the lady's room when Paul entered from the terrace. And loveliest sight of all, in front of the fire, stretched at full length, was his tiger [skin] – and on him – also at full length – reclined the lady, garbed in some strange clinging garments of heavy purple crêpe, its hem embroidered with gold, one white arm resting on the beast's head, her back supported by a pile of the velvet cushions, and a heap of rarely bound books at her side, while between her red lips was a rose not redder than they – an almost scarlet rose. Paul had never seen one as red before.

The whole picture was barbaric. It might have been some painter's dream of the Favourite in a harem. It was not what one would expect to find in a sedate Swiss hotel.

From *Three Weeks*, 1907 | Elinor Glyn (1864–1553)

No pen could possibly do justice to the exquisite charm and beauty of Maria's room. It was at the top of the tower, and the tower was a round one, so Maria's room was circular, neither too large nor too small, just the right size for a girl of thirteen...

There was no carpet upon the silvery-oak floor, but a little white sheepskin lay beside the bed, so that Maria's bare toes should meet something warm and soft when they went floorwards of a morning. The bed was a little four-poster, hung with pale-blue silk curtains embroidered with silver stars, of the same material as the window curtains, and spread with a patchwork quilt made of exquisite squares of velvet and silk of all colours of the rainbow, gay and lovely.

There was very little furniture in the room, just a couple of silvery-oak chests for Maria's clothes, a small round mirror hung upon the wall above one of them, and a stool with a silver ewer and basin upon it. But Maria felt that she wanted no more than this...

...Standing there so slender and straight in her grey dress, her room seemed to curve itself about her like the petals of a flower about its heart; they completed each other.

From *The Little White Horse*, 1946 | Elizabeth Goudge (1900–1984)

At the age of eight years, I was very desirous of acquiring the use of my needle; but my parents discouraged the idea, thinking it wholly impractical. I was not, however, intimidated, and whenever my father and mother were absent, I was continually practising every invention, 'til at length I could, with my mouth – thread a needle – tie a knot – do fancy work – cut out and make my own dresses.

Sarah Biffin, *disabled professional miniaturist who signed her work 'painted by Miss Biffin Without Hands'* (1781–1850)

What is a Superwoman? The answer is simple. She is not a woman who can do anything but a woman who avoids trying to do too much. She knows her own limitations and sticks happily within them; she realises that Life is untidy and so are the children in it...

...Naturally, a Superwoman does as little housework as possible and this can be quite difficult; you have to be well organised to keep it in its place, which, as far as I'm concerned, is firmly underfoot. Good organization doesn't just happen naturally, any more than good sex. You have to learn how to do it and then put in a lot of practice, like the piano.

Another good reason for avoiding housework is in order to have more time for yourself. Because, as well as being the supporting cast of the entire family show, YOU ARE THE ONE AND ONLY STAR OF YOUR OWN LIFE.

From *Superwoman in Action*, 1979 | Shirley Conran (1932–2024)

A happy life is one spent in learning, earning and yearning.

Lilian Gish (1893–1993)

'Do you seriously intend to stay here all your life? To wash dishes that the next meal will soil, to arrange flowers that will wither in a week, to walk in fear and trembling of what Mrs Marshall Gurney will say, although you know quite well that she hasn't got the intelligence to say anything worth saying?'...

'We can't all be clever,' she said, without much joy in the thought.

'Clever? Who said that we all had to be clever? But we have to have courage. The whole position of women is what it is to-day, because so many of us have followed the line of least resistance, and have sat down placidly in a little provincial town, waiting to get married.'

From *The Crowded Street*, 1924 | Winfred Holtby (1898–1935)

[When travelling] You step from one life into another. You are yourself, but a different self. The new self is untrammelled by all the hundreds of spiders' webs and filaments that enclose you in a cocoon of day-to-day domestic life: letters to write and bills to pay, chores to do, friends to see, photographs to develop, clothes to mend, nurses and servants to placate, tradesmen and laundries to reprove. Your travel life has the essence of a dream. It is something outside the normal, yet you are in it. It is peopled with characters you have never seen before and in all probability will never see again.

From *An Autobiography*, 1977 | Agatha Christie (1890–1976)

There were legions of her kind during the nineteen-thirties, women from the age of thirty and upward, who crowded their war-bereaved spinsterhood with voyages of discovery into new ideas and energetic practices in art or social welfare, education or religion... They went to lectures, tried living on honey and nuts, took lessons in German and then went walking in Germany; they bought caravans and then went off with them into the hills among the lochs; they played the guitar, they supported all the new little theatre companies; they took lodgings in the slums and, distributing pots of paint, taught their neighbours the arts of simple interior decoration; they preached the inventions of Marie Stopes; they attended the meetings of the Oxford Group and put spiritualism to their hawk-eyed test.

From *The Prime of Miss Jean Brodie*, 1961 | Muriel Spark (1918–2006)

The women never worked in the vegetable gardens or on the allotments, even when they had their children off hand and had plenty of spare time, for there was strict division of labour and that was 'men's work'... But even that code permitted a woman to cultivate a flower garden, and most of the houses had at least a narrow border beside the pathway... pinks and sweet williams and love-in-a-mist, wallflowers and forget-me-nots in spring and hollyhocks and Michaelmas daisies in autumn.

From *Lark Rise to Candleford*, 1949 | Flora Thompson (1876–1947)

The work in the vegetables – Gertrude Stein was undertaking for the moment the care of the flowers and box hedges – was a full-time job and more. Later it became a joke, Gertrude Stein asking me what I saw when I closed my eyes, and I answered, weeds. That, she said, was not the answer, and so weeds were changed to strawberries. The small strawberries, called by the French wood strawberries, are not wild but cultivated. It took me an hour to gather a small basket for Gertrude Stein's breakfast, and later when there was a plantation of them in the upper garden our young guests were told that if they cared to eat them they should do the picking themselves.

The first gathering of the garden in May of salads, radishes and herbs made me feel like a mother about her baby – how could anything so beautiful be mine. And this emotion of wonder filled me for each vegetable as it was gathered every year. There is nothing that is comparable to it, as satisfactory or as thrilling, as gathering the vegetables one has grown.

From *The Alice B Toklas Cook Book*, 1954 | Alice B. Toklas (1877–1967)

A really long day of weeding is a restful experience, and quite changes the current of thought. For some people it is more efficient than a rest cure. It is pleasantest to take a nine-hour day of such work when the earth is wet, or even in rain, because weeds come up more easily, root and branch, from wet earth. I never want an hour at noon for dinner, like the hired man, but would prefer to lunch like horses from a nosebag. It would save time, and especially the necessity of cleaning oneself. After such a day my fingers are bleeding, knees tottering, back bent, dress muddy and soaking, and shoes an offence to my tidy maid; but I have attained the most profound inward peace, and the blessed belief of having uprooted all my enemies.

From *An Artist's Garden*, 1908 | Anna Lea Merritt (1844–1930)

I wrote the 21st letter to Alan today [her son, taken prisoner at Dunkirk], and just for a few moments this evening black depression flooded over me...

And then one's spirits just had to rise in the garden and one thought of the queer things one was thankful for personally – such varied things as the five tall cypresses on the lawn, so handsome; the bronze green of the yew hedge in the fading light, the colour of colours; a new thumbnail just grown to perfection after nearly a year; the feel of newly-cut hair and the blessing of a permanent wave; one's good bed; the rain and the sun; autumn colouring; good garden tools and a wickerwork barrow; the way Twink's ears fall and his easy action; and a thousand other things day by day. And then for one's good friends and most of all for the nearest and dearest – and home.

Diary entry, 6 October 1940, from *Mrs Milburn's Diaries*, 1979 | Clara Milburn (1883–1961)

All the same I am not going to accept your kind invitation, for the time being at any rate. The reason is that my pink cactus is probably going to flower. It is a very rare plant I've been given, and I'm told that in our climate it flowers only once every four years. Now, I am already a very old woman, and if I went away when my pink cactus was going to flower, I am certain I shouldn't see it flower again.

Colette (1873–1954) to her son-in-law

I woke to the sun on a daffodil. I had put a bunch of daffodils and purple tulips on the bureau and when I woke the sun hit just one daffodil, a single beam on the yellow frilled cup and outer petals. After a bad night the sight got me up and going.

Diary entry, 4 February 1971, from *Journal of a Solitude*, 1973 | May Sarton (1912–1995)

The treasures in the garden now are all tiny - blue wood anemones in a small carpet round the viburnum are a great success; the fritillaries with their strange chequered bells have done well under the forsythia; leucojum, those large white bells, each with a tiny green spot drawn on the petals (like a child's drawing of an imaginary flower) are thriving; the white violets with a fine blue stripe at the throat are out too - and I am furious at having to be away these days. The changes come so fast. I want to be here.

Diary entry, 20 May 1971, from *Journal of a Solitude*, 1973 | May Sarton (1912–1995)

From *The Bluebell*

There is a silent eloquence
In every wild bluebell
That fills my softened heart with bliss
That words could never tell.

Anne Brontë (1820–1849)

Mrs Arbuthnot said nothing to that for two reasons, - first, because she was struck by the remarkable and growing calm of the hitherto incoherent and excited Lotty, and secondly because what she was looking at was so very beautiful.

All down the stone steps on either side were periwinkles in full flower, and she could now see what it was that had caught at her the night before and brushed, wet and scented, across her face. It was wisteria. Wisteria and sunshine ... Colour seemed flung down anyhow, anywhere; every sort of colour, piled up in heaps, pouring along in rivers - the periwinkles looked exactly as if they were being poured down each side of the steps - and flowers that grew only in borders in England, proud flowers keeping themselves to themselves over there, such as the great blue irises and the lavender, were being jostled by small, shining common things like dandelions and daisies and the white bells of the wild onion, and only seemed the better and the more exuberant for it.

They stood looking at this crowd of loveliness, this happy jumble, in silence. No, it didn't matter what Mrs Fisher did; not here; not in such beauty. Mrs Arbuthnot's discomposure melted out of her. In the warmth and light of what she was looking at, of what to her was a manifestation, an entirely new side, of God, how could one be discomposed? If only Frederick were with her, seeing it too, seeing as he would have seen it when first they were lovers, in the days when he saw what she saw and loved what she loved...

She sighed.

'You mustn't sigh in heaven,' said Mrs Wilkins. 'One doesn't.'

From *The Enchanted April*, 1922 | Elizabeth von Arnim (1866–1941)

Beside him on the gallery, Sidda and Connor looked down on the garden, a wild profusion of blooming begonias, impatiens, and the remnants of big, showy caladium leaves. The sweet scent of butterfly ginger, its white flowers glowing in the darkness, reached up to greet them. Surrounded by the tangled masses of Spanish moss hanging from giant live oaks, the garden was enclosed by old brick walls, which were covered by a few remaining Rose of Montana blossoms. A fountain with a small pool sat in the far corner of the garden, buttressed on one side by a chinaberry tree and on the other by a crepe myrtle, its leaves gold and red with autumn. Lush plantings of a variety of camellias, azaleas, roses of all kinds, salvias, and jasmine filled the space so completely that the red brick floor of the courtyard was barely visible.

Sidda looked at the huge camellia bush, its buds full and swollen. 'I never knew Buggy – that's what we called my grandmother – was such a great gardener,' Sidda said.

From *Divine Secrets of the Ya-Ya Sisterhood*, 1996 | Rebecca Wells (b.1952)

'It is all different already,' she said. 'The grass is greener and things are sticking up everywhere and things are uncurling and green buds of leaves are showing. This afternoon I am sure Dickon will come.'

The long warm rain had done strange things to the herbaceous beds which bordered the walk by the lower wall. There were things sprouting and pushing out from the roots of clumps of plants and there were actually here and there glimpses of royal purple and yellow unfurling among the stems of crocuses. Six months before Mistress Mary would not have seen how the world was waking up, but now she missed nothing.

From *The Secret Garden*, 1911 | Frances Hodgson Burnett (1849–1924)

Outside in the garden which was full of mellow sunset lights streaming through the dark old firs to the west of it, stood Anne and Diana, gazing bashfully at one another over a clump of gorgeous tiger lilies.

The Barry garden was a bowery wilderness of flowers which would have delighted Anne's heart at any time less fraught with destiny. It was encircled by huge old willows and tall fruits, beneath which flourished flowers that loved the shade. Prim, right-angled paths, neatly bordered with clam-shells, intersected it like moist red ribbons, and in the beds between old-fashioned flowers ran riot. There were rosy bleeding-hearts and great splendid crimson peonies; white, fragrant narcissi and thorny, sweet Scotch roses; pink and blue and white columbines and lilac-tinted Bouncing

Bets; clumps of southernwood and ribbon grass and mint; purple Adam-and-Eve, daffodils, and masses of sweet clover white with its delicate, fragrant, feathery sprays; scarlet lightning that shot its fiery lances over prim white musk-flowers; a garden it was where sunshine lingered and bees hummed, and winds, beguiled into loitering, purred and rustled.

'Oh, Diana,' said Anne at last, clasping her hands and speaking almost in a whisper, 'do you think – oh, do you think you can like me a little – enough to be my bosom friend?'

Diana laughed. Diana always laughed before she spoke.

'Why, I guess so,' she said frankly.

From *Anne of Green Gables*, 1908 | L M Montgomery (1874–1942)

There were flowers: delphiniums, sweet peas, bunches of delphiniums and carnations, masses of carnations. There were roses, there were irises. Ah yes – so she breathed in in the earthy-garden sweet smell as she stood talking to Miss Pym who owed her help, and thought her kind, for kind she had been years ago; very kind, but she looked older, this year, turning her head from side to side among the irises and roses and nodding tufts of lilac with her eyes half closed snuffing in, after the street uproar, the delicious scent, the exquisite coolness. And then, opening her eyes, how fresh, like frilled linen clean from a laundry laid in wicker trays, the roses looked; and dark and prim the red carnations, holding their heads up; and all the sweet peas spreading in their bowls, tinged violet, snow white, pale – as if it were the evening and girls in muslin frocks came out to pick sweet peas and roses after the superb summer's day, with its almost blue-black sky, its delphiniums, its carnations, its arum lilies was over; and it was the moment between six and seven when every flower – roses, carnations, irises, lilac – glows...

And as she began to go with Miss Pym from jar to jar, choosing, nonsense, nonsense, she said to herself, more and more gently, as if this beauty, this scent, this colour, and Miss Pym liking her, trusting her, were a wave which she left flow over her and surmount that hatred, that monster, surmount it all; and it lifted her up and up when – oh! a pistol shot in the street outside.

From *Mrs Dalloway*, 1925 | Virginia Woolf (1882–1941)

'What is it, Sadie?' Laura came into the hall.

'It's the florist, Miss Laura.'

It was, indeed. There. Just inside the door, stood a wide, shallow tray full of pots of pink lilies. No other kind. Nothing but lilies – canna lilies, big pink flowers, wide open, radiant, almost frighteningly alive on bright crimson stems.

'O-oh, Sadie!' said Laura, and the sound was like a little moan. She crouched down as if to warm herself at that blaze of lilies; she felt they were in her fingers, on her lips, growing in her breast.

'It's some mistake,' she said faintly. 'Nobody ever ordered so many. Sadie, go and find mother.'

But at that moment Mrs Sheridan joined them.

'It's quite right,' she said calmly. 'Yes, I ordered them. Aren't they lovely?' She pressed Laura's arm. 'I was passing the shop yesterday, and I saw them in the window. And I suddenly thought for once in my life I shall have enough canna lilies. The garden party will be a good excuse.'

From 'The Garden Party', 1922 | Katherine Mansfield (1888–1923)

...the Dahlia's first duty in life is to flaunt and to swagger and to carry gorgeous blooms well above its leaves, and on no account to hang its head.

From *Wood and Garden*, 1899 | Gertrude Jekyll (1843–1932)

I have very often deprived myself of the necessities of life, but I have never consented to give up a luxury.

Colette (1873–1954) to the Countess Anna de Noailles, June 1812

Gather here - all who have passion and who desire to create new conditions of life - new visions of art and literature and new magic worlds of poetry and music. If I could but feel that days at Garsington had strengthened your efforts to live the noble life, to live freely, recklessly, with clear Reason released from convention - no longer absorbed in small personal events but valuing personal affair as part of a great whole - above all to live with passionate desire for Truth and Love and Understanding and Imagination.

Lady Ottoline Morrell (1873–1958) on Garsington Manor, c.1914

Travel, trouble, music, art,
A kiss, a frock, a rhyme, -
I never said they feed my heart,
But still, they pass my time.

From *Enough Rope*, 1926 | Dorothy Parker (1893–1967)

Things I like: firs, Venice, tequila, sunsets, babies, silent films, heights, coarse salt, large long-haired dogs, ship models, cinnamon, goose down quilts, pocket watches, the smell of newly mown grass, linen, Bach, Louis XIII furniture, sushi, microscopes, large rooms, ups, boots, drinking water, maple sugar candy...

Things I like: drums, carnations, socks, raw peas, chewing on sugar cane, bridges, Dürer, escalators, hot weather, sturgeon, tall people, deserts, white walls, horses, electric typewriters, cherries, wicker/rattan furniture, sitting cross-legged, stripes, large windows, fresh dill, reading aloud, going to bookstores, under-furnished rooms, dancing, Ariadne auf Naxos.

Diary entry, 21 February 1977, from *As Consciousness is Harnessed to Flesh*, 2012 | Susan Sontag (1933–2004)

I became obsessed with my electric bicycle. I had wheels. One night I rode to a party at least twenty miles away. I whizzed along the roads with my dress flying in the wind behind me. It was hard not to whoop. Perhaps my children and my e-bike were my only happiness...

My e-bike was more demanding than my children. Earlier, on my way to the meeting, two different men had stopped to ask about my e-bike, one at the traffic lights in Camden Town, one by the fruit stall outside Goodge Street station. ... I was the minor character and the e-bike was a countercultural celebrity. I suppose the men were minor characters and I had stepped outside my character, happy to explain that the maximum assisted speed was 15mph and it was fitted with a motor of 200 watts. While I talked to them, I felt I had joined a kind of brotherhood, while at the same time struggling with motherhood. I was an e-matriarch in a patriarchal reality.

From *The Cost of Living*, 2018 | Deborah Levy (b.1959)

Only is the sunlight ever normal at Garsington? No, I think even the sky is done up in pale yellow silk, and certainly the cabbages are scented.

Vanessa Bell (1879–1961) to Barbara Bagenal, 24 June 1923

Dearest David,
...Tiber makes love to you for the good reason that he loves you, and loves making love. Cats are passionate and voluptuous... I am so glad you have each other. Does he roll on his head? Does he fall asleep with an ownerly paw laid over you?
We had a dark grey cat (Norfolk bred, very Norfolk in character) called Tom. He was reserved, domineering, voluptuous – much as I imagine Tiber to be. When he was middle-aged he gave up nocturnal prowling and slept on my bed, against my feet. One evening I was reading in bed when I became aware that Tom was staring at me. I put down my book, said nothing, watched. Slowly, with a look of intense concentration, he advanced on me, like Tarquin with ravishing strides, poised himself, put out a front paw, and stroked my cheek as I used to stroke his chops. A human caress from a cat. I felt very meagre and ill-educated that I could not purr.

Sylvia Townsend Warner (1893–1978) to David Garnett, 18 June 1973

I'm sitting in the office of a well-respected casting director in New York, making amiable conversation and desperately trying not to bleed through to this woman's couch. The meeting had swiftly taken a turn for the better when I reached for my conversational jackpot piece and struck gold – the casting director was also a cat lady.

Her eyes lit up as I mentioned how I flew my beloved sidekick, a precious Persian by the name of Puff, across the ocean to room with me for two months in New York City. It's a risky move, mentioning a cat in this environment, when statistically, a career womn living in New York is much more likely to have a dog (office-trained, travels well, the size of a small bag of groceries) and if she does, she will swiftly judge me and end the meeting sooner than anticipated, or worse, she will feel my own irrepressible disdain for dog people and I will never hear from her again. But, oh joy, she has a cat! Two cats, in fact!

Suddenly, we are gal pals. Suddenly, I feel rays of light emanating from my career prospects, which have just brightened considerably. We will make movies together, Mrs Reputable New-York-City Casting Lady and I! She will think of me when casting her next quirky independent rom-com and I'll audition, winningly, and afterwards she'll ask, 'How is your sweet, sweet cat?'

From 'Cat Women' in *Feminists Don't Wear Pink (and other lies)*, curated by Scarlett Curtis, 2018 | Evanna Lynch (b.1991)

My little dog seemed to know I was late: he ran eagerly to me and frolicked round my feet, as if glad I'd come at last. Suddenly, he began to cough, a queer hard cough, and collapsed on his side. I thought he was dead. As I knelt and gently stroked him, it came to me with a painful shock that soon my little friend and I must part. He is turned thirteen, and showing signs of ageing quickly. To me, he is more than an animal: he has kindness, understanding and intelligence, and not only knows all that is said, but often reads my mind to an uncanny degree. He knows when I'm sad and dim, and lies with his head on my foot, or follows me closely about as if to say, 'I cannot help you, but please understand I love you and will stand by.' As I stroked him, and spoke soothingly, his little stumpy tail wagged feebly, his eyes opened and he looked up as if to say, 'Don't worry, I'll be alright soon.'

Diary entry, 10 November 1942, *Nella Last's War*, 2007 | Nella Last (1889–1968)

My little cats rushed to meet me as if I'd been away for a week. Mrs Newall and I sat in a corner to have our tea and I hastily slipped the bit of chicken skin and a wee bone into an envelope when no one was looking, wishing I'd the courage to offer to buy a few kitchen scraps for my little friends. Their delight was comical to see...

Diary entry, 5 November 1946, from *Nella Last's Peace*, 2008 | Nella Last (1889–1968)

So in the beginning of February I began privately to prepare Six Designs, taking for my Model that charming rascal Benjamin Bouncer our tame Jack Hare – I may mention (better the day better the deed) that my best designs occurred to me in chapel – I was rather impeded by the inquisitiveness of my aunt, and the idiosyncrasies of Benjamin who has an appetite for certain sorts of paint, but the cards were finished by Easter [*and eventually accepted for publication*]...

My first act was to give Bounce (what an investment that rabbit has been in spite of the hutches), a cupful of hemp seeds, the consequence being that when I wanted to draw him next morning he was partially intoxicated and wholly unmanageable.

Then I retired to bed, and lay awake chuckling till 2 in the morning, and afterwards had an impression that Bunny came to my bedside in a white cotton night cap and tickled me with his whiskers.

Diary entry, May 1890 | Beatrix Potter (1866–1943)

Madame, in accordance with the letter you have written me I send you a greyhound which is one of the best I have been able to procure in this town at present, trusting that in good time I shall be able to send you some others, as also for my lord your son some water-spaniels which I shall send to England to procure, as in this town [Calais] one can hardly come by them, which is the cause why I send to my lord your son at present only one such water-dog. But I ensure you, and your son also, that he cannot have had many better in his time. He knoweth well how to retrieve the head or the bolt of a crossbow, as well by water as on land, or other such things as one willeth him to seek, and if one holdeth on high a piece of cloth or a glove on the end of a stick, he will go seek them and hath many another trick that he can perform.

Lady Lisle (1493–1556) to Madame de Bours, 28 February 1549

"I want to ride my horse in the Grand National. I want to race against the best in the world, and I want to win!"

From *National Velvet*, 1935 | Enid Bagnold (1889–1991)

Horses lend us the wings we lack.

Pam Brown, *Australian poet* (b.1948)

One day, when there was a good deal of kicking, my mother whinnied to me to come to her, and then she said:

'I wish you to pay attention to what I am going to say to you. The colts who live here are very good colts, but they are cart-horse colts, and of course they have not learned manners. You have been well-bred and well-born; your father has a great name in these parts; and your grandfather won the cup two years at the Newmarket races; your grandmother had the sweetest temper of any horse I ever knew, and I think you have never seen me kick or bite. I hope you will grow up gentle and good, and never learn bad ways; do your work with a good will, lift your feet up well when you trot, and never bite or kick even in play.'

I have never forgotten my mother's advice; I knew she was a wise old horse...

From *Black Beauty*, 1877 | Anna Sewell (1820–1878)

It was a threatening misty morning - but mild. We set off after dinner from Eusemere... When we were in the woods beyond Gowsbarrow park we saw a few daffodils close to the water side. We fancied that the lake had floated the seeds ashore and that the little colony had so sprung up. But as we went along there were more and yet more and at last under the boughs of the trees, we saw that there was a long belt of them along the shore, about the breadth of a country turnpike road. I never saw daffodils so beautiful they grew among the mossy stones about and about them, some rested their heads upon these stones as on a pillow for weariness and the rest tossed and reeled and danced and seemed as if they verily laughed with the wind that blew upon them over the lake, they looked so gay ever glancing ever changing.

Diary entry, 15 April 1802 (*two years before her brother William wrote his famous poem, 'I Wandered Lonely as A Cloud'*) | Dorothy Wordsworth (1771–1855)

Chapter 8

FUTURES AND FAITH

FUTURES AND FAITH

All shall be well, and all shall be well, and all manner of things shall be well.

From *Revelations of Divine Love*, 1670 | Julian of Norwich, *anchoress and mystic* (c.1342–after 1416)

The future belongs to those who believe in the beauty of their dreams.

Eleanor Roosevelt (1884–1962)

Everyone has oceans to fly, if they have the heart to do it. Is it reckless? Maybe. But what do dreams know of boundaries?

Amelia Earhart (1897–1937)

When she stopped conforming to the conventional picture of femininity, she finally began to enjoy being a woman.

From *The Feminine Mystique*, 1963 | Betty Friedan (1921–2006)

I am the Queen, the gatherer-up of treasures, the most thoughtful, first of those who merit worship.

Thus gods have established me in many places with many homes to enter and abide in.

Through me alone all eat the food that feeds them, – each man who sees, breathes, hears the word outspoken

They know it not, yet I reside in the essence of the Universe. Hear, one and all, the truth as I declare it.

I, verily, myself announce and utter the word that gods and men alike shall welcome.

I make the man I love exceeding mighty, make him nourished, a sage, and one who knows Brahman. I bend the bow for Rudra that his arrow may strike and slay the hater of devotion.

I rouse and order battle for the people, I created Earth and Heaven and reside as their inner controller.

On the world's summit I bring forth the Father: my home is in the waters, in the ocean.

Thence I pervade all existing creatures, as their Inner Supreme Self, and manifest them with my body.

I created all worlds at my will, without any higher being, and permeate and dwell within them.

The eternal and infinite consciousness is I, it is my greatness dwelling in everything.

From 'Devi Suktam', a hymn from the Sanskrit Rigveda, often attributed to a woman scholar, or Brahmavadini, 1500–1000BC

From this mighty storehouse (of God, and the hierarchies of Spiritual Beings) we may gather wisdom and knowledge, and receive light and power, as we pass through this preparatory room of earth, which is only one of the innumerable mansions in our Father's house. Think on these things.

From *The Worlds and I*, 1918 | Ella Wheeler Wilcox (1850–1919)

She was created in the image of God! How can anyone dare slander the vessel that bears such a noble imprint? ...And if anyone says that it was a woman, Lady Eve, who caused man's fall from Paradise, I would say that man gained more through Mary than he lost through Eve.

From *The Book of the City of Ladies*, 1405 | Christine de Pizan (1364–1431)

A happy life is the perfect life to which we are lead by a firm faith, cheerful hope, and fervent love.

St Monica of Tagaste (c.331–387 AD), quoted by her son St Augustine in his *De Vita Beata*, 386 AD

It was undoubtedly a fact that faith was failing. Nowadays, at the moment of getting into bed, when a lifetime's habit still suggested prayer, one's immediate reaction was a confused mental protest, like an impatient shrug of scepticism; and straightaway, a shade uneasy, into bed one got and thought about something else...

Oh, but it can't be helped! It'll all come right. Because, of course, I do believe... I believe – I believe in everything... sun, moon, stars, in seasons – trees, flowers – people, music, life... yes, in life. She was shaken with excitement, took a deep breath...

From, *Invitation to the Waltz*, 1932 | Rosamond Lehmann (1901–1990)

What is so nice & so unexpected about life is the way it improves as it goes along. I think you should impress this fact on your children because I think young people have an awful feeling that life is slipping past them & they must do something – catch something – they don't quite know what, whereas they've only got to wait and it all comes.

Nancy Mitford (1904–1973)

I want every girl to know that her voice can change the world.

Malala Yousafzai (b.1997)

Through the miracle of publishing, I have had three of my childhood fantasies fulfilled.

First of all, the six-year-old in me was astonished to find that I had been encapsulated in the humor section of Reader's Digest. More precisely, several excerpts from my books have been used in the 'Quotable Quotes' section.

You have to realise that Reader's Digest was the only magazine to which my parents subscribed...

A second childhood fantasy was fulfilled when I made it into a 'Women We Love' issue of *Esquire* shortly after I was first published. I had my picture taken by a Famous Photographer. This was a great achievement to the fifteen-year-old version of myself, who still inhabits a portion of my body, which in my memory of adolescence was lumpy, distorted, perhaps even bordering on disfigured. When the issue of *Esquire* appeared on the stands, I wanted to track down all the boys who'd been at school with me at Peterson High in Sunnyvale and show them: 'See? That's me. Bet you're sorry now that you never asked me to dance.' Pathetic, I know.

My third and crowning fantasy-come-true was an appearance in *Playboy*. Years and years ago, I used to fret that my Maidenform held no maidenly forms. I would press my palms at chest level to inflate my pectorals isometrically. I bought creams that promised to increase the bust by at least one of two inches. Nothing worked, and like those who've bought useless Viagra-like pills nowadays, I was too mortified to file for my money-back guarantee. So imagine my surprise when I appeared in *Playboy* as a dominatrix in black leather and chains.

All right, so I am only one tiny character in a cartoon of the entire band The Rock Bottom Remainders, humorously rendered along with Stephen King, Dave Barry, and Barbara Kingsolver. But through the cartoonist's sweep of the pen, certain aspects of my persona have been generously enhanced, no surgeon's knife necessary. At last I have a figure with eye-popping cleavage good enough for *Playboy*.

From *The Opposite of Fate*, 2001 | Amy Tan (b.1952)

Who wants to become a writer? And why? ...It's the streaming reason for living. To note, to pin down, to build up, to create, to be astonished at nothing, to cherish the oddities, to let nothing go down the drain, to make something, to make a great flower of life, even if it's a cactus.

Enid Bagnold (1889–1981)

We do not have to become heroes overnight. Just a step at a time, meeting each thing that comes up, seeing it is not as dreadful as it appears, discovering that we have the strength to stare it down.

Eleanor Roosevelt (1884–1962)

It's sad to grow old, but nice to ripen.

Brigitte Bardot (b.1934)

You can be gorgeous at thirty, charming at forty, and irresistible for the rest of your life.

Coco Chanel (1883–1971)

Woman is learning for herself that not self-sacrifice, but self-development, is her first duty in life; and this, not primarily for the sake of others but that she may become fully herself.

Matilda Joslyn Gage (1826–1898)

Please don't retouch my wrinkles. It took me so long to earn them.

Anna Magnani (1908–1973) to a photographer

A First Lady's power is a curious thing - as soft and undefined as the role itself. And yet I was learning to harness it. I had no executive authority. I didn't command troops or engage in formal diplomacy. Tradition called for me to provide a kind of gentle light, flattering the president with my devotion, flattering the nation primarily by not challenging it. I was beginning to see, though, that wielded carefully the light was more powerful than that. I had influence in the form of being something of a curiosity - a Black First Lady, a professional woman, a mother of young kids. People seemed to want to dial into my clothes, my shoes, and my hairstyles, but they also had to see me in the context of what I was and why. I was learning to connect my message to my image, and in this way I could direct the American gaze...

It was a revelation. All of it was a revelation. With my soft power, I was finding I could be strong.

From *Becoming*, 2018 | Michelle Obama (b. 1964)

Because the true test of courage is to be afraid and go ahead and do it anyway. To be scared, to have your knees knocking, but to walk on in there anyway.

From *Oprah Winfrey Speaks*, Janet Lowe, 2001 | Oprah Winfrey (b.1954)

To
a small girl child
who may live to grasp
somewhat of that which for
us
is yet sight, not touch.

From *Dreams*, 1890 | Olive Schreiner (1855–1920)

Flops are a part of life's menu and I've never been a girl to miss out on any of the courses.

From *New York Herald Tribune*, 11 April 1957 | Rosalind Russell (1907–1976)

And Still I Rise

You may write me down in history
With your bitter, twisted lies,
You may trod me in the very dirt
But still, like dust, I'll rise.

Does my sassiness upset you?
Why are you beset with gloom?
'Cause I walk like I've got oil wells
Pumping in my living room.
Just like moons and like suns,
With the certainty of tides,
Just like hopes springing high,
Still I'll rise.

Did you want to see me broken?

Bowed head and lowered eyes?
Shoulders falling down like teardrops,
Lowered by my soulful cries?

Does my haughtiness offend you?
Don't you take it awful hard
'Cause I laugh like I've got gold mines
Diggin' in my own back yard.

You may shoot me with your words,
You may cut me with your eyes,
You may kill me with your hatefulness
But still, like air, I'll rise.

Does my sexiness upset you?
Does it come as a surprise
That I dance like I've got diamonds
At the meeting of my thighs?

Out of the huts of history's shame
I rise
Up from a past that's rooted in pain
I rise
I'm a black ocean, leaping and wide,
Welling and swelling I bear in the tide.

Leaving behind nights of terror and fear
I rise
Into a daybreak that's wondrously clear
I rise

Bringing the gifts that my ancestors gave,
I am the dream and the hope of the slave
I rise
I rise
I rise.

Maya Angelou (1928–2014)

Just returned from a week in San Francisco with Robert. Extraordinary trip...

Two interesting visions occurred when we were together: I had a vision of us slaying dragons – back to back, swords flashing. Then off we went to glide down a river in a canoe. My hand trailing in the water.

Then, when I was listening to Stevie Wonder with Robert & hearing the song 'As' – 'I'll be loving you *always*' I saw, not Robert or anybody else. Just *myself*. Alice loving Alice. Kissing Alice. Embracing Alice. Dancing all around the world with Alice. This self-love and self-generated joy continued through the other songs.

It is true. I do love myself. I accept myself. I take myself to my bosom. I feel such tenderness for myself, often so lost, confused. Struggling.

Diary entry, 3 February 1978, from *Gathering Blossoms Under Fire*, 2022 | Alice Walker (b.1944)

I wish I knew what people mean when they say they find 'emptiness' in this wonderful adventure of living, which seems to me to pile up its glories like an horizon-wide sunset as the light declines. I'm afraid I'm an incorrigible life-lover & life-wonderer & adventurer.

Edith Wharton (1862–1937) to Mary Berenson, 11 October 1936

Sympathy

There should be no despair for you
While nightly stars are burning;
While evening pours its silent dew
And sunshine guilds the morning.
There should be no despair – though tears
May flow down like a river:
Art not the best beloved of years
Around your heart forever?

They weep, you weep, it must be so;
Winds sigh as you are sighing,
And Winter sheds his grief in snow
Where Autumn's leaves are lying:
Yet, these revive, and from their fate
Your fate cannot be parted:
Then, journey on, if not elate,
Still, never broken-hearted!

'Ellis Bell' (Emily Brontë) (1818–1848)

I do not wish [women] to have power over men, but over themselves.

From *A Vindication of the Rights of Woman*, 1792 | Mary Wollstonecraft (1759–1797)

I told you in the course of this paper that Shakespeare had a sister; but do not look for her in Sir Sidney Lee's life of the poet. She died young – alas, she never wrote a word. She lies buried where the omnibuses now stop, opposite the Elephant and Castle. Now my belief is that this poet who never wrote a word and was buried at the crossroads still lives. She lives in you and in me, and in many other women who are not here tonight, for they are washing up the dishes and putting the children to bed. But she lives; for great poets do not die; they need only the opportunity to walk among us in the flesh. This opportunity, as I think, it is now coming within your power to give her. For my belief is that if we live another century or so... the opportunity will come and the dead poet who was Shakespeare's sister will put on the body which she has so often laid down. Drawing her life from the lives of the unknown who were her forerunners, as her brother did before her, she will be born.

From *A Room of One's Own*, 1929 | Virginia Woolf (1882–1941)

I believe in laughter. I believe in friends. I believe in wine. I believe in crisps. I believe in coffee. I believe in art. I believe in beauty. I believe in grace. I believe in kindness. I believe in wit. I believe in doubt. I believe in cake. I believe in moving your body, since it's the only one you get. I believe in hard work. I believe in lie-ins. I believe in candles, and canapés, and champagne. I believe that the world works an awful lot better if people are nice. I believe there are usually some reasons to be cheerful, but sometimes it would be weird not to feel sad. I believe in learning. I believe in curiosity. Oh my God, I believe in curiosity. I believe it's the best way to remind ourselves that we're tiny specks in a big world. And believe in anger. Yes, I do believe in anger, but the kind of anger that gives you the energy to fight back.

From *The Art of Not Falling Apart*, 2019 | Christina Patterson (b.1963)

I keep remembering one of my Guru's teachings about happiness. She said that people universally tend to think that happiness is a stroke of luck, something that will maybe descend upon you like fine weather if you're fortunate enough. But that's not how happiness works. Happiness is the consequence of personal effort. You fight for it, strive for it, insist upon it, and sometimes even travel around the world looking for it. You have to participate relentlessly in the manifestations of your own blessings. And once you have achieved a state of happiness, you must never become lax about maintaining it, you must make a mighty effort to keep swimming upward into that happiness forever, to stay afloat on top of it. If you don't, you will leak away your innate contentment. It's easy enough to pray when you're in distress but continuing to pray even when your crisis has passed is like a sealing process, helping your soul hold tight to its good attainments.

From *Eat, Pray, Love*, 2006 | Elizabeth Gilbert (b.1969)

Some of us have great runways already built for us. If you have one, take off. But if you don't have one, realize it is your responsibility to grab a shovel and build one for yourself and for those who will follow after you.

Amelia Earhart (1897–1937)

Women, like men, should try to do the impossible. And when they fail, their failure should be a challenge to others.

Amelia Earhart (1897–1937)

To the doubters and naysayers and everyone who gave me hell and said I could not, that I would not, or I must not – your resistance made me stronger, made me push harder, and made me the fighter that I am today. It made me the woman that I am today. So, thank you.

Madonna (b.1958)

There is no greater power in the world than the zest of a post-menopausal woman.

Margaret Mead (1901–1978)

As women achieve power, the barriers will fall. As society sees what women can do, as women see what women can do, there will be more women out there doing things, and we'll all be better off for it.

Ruth Bader Ginsburg (1933–2020)

You don't get to decide how you are going to die or when. You can only decide how you're going to live.

From *Daybreak: An Intimate Journal*, 1968 | Joan Baez (b.1941)

I feel I must fight for [my music] because I want women to turn their minds to big and difficult jobs; not just to go on hugging the shore, afraid to put out to sea.

Ethel Smyth (1858–1944)

Be sure to live in vain, dear. I wish I had.

Emily Dickinson (1830–1886) to her niece Mattie

It was done; it was finished. Yes, she thought, laying down her brush in extreme fatigue, I have had my vision.

From *To the Lighthouse*, 1927 | Virginia Woolf (1882–1941)

It is good to have an end to journey towards; but it is the journey that matters, in the end.

From *The Left Hand of Darkness*, 1969 | Ursula K Le Guin (1929–2018)

I love my past, I love my present. I am not ashamed of what I have had, and I am not sad because I no longer have it.

From *The Last of Chéri*, 1926 | Colette (1873–1954)

Wednesday 9 March [2016]
I'm back to work full-time today, and it does feel very different compared to returning for just a few days at a time between chemo sessions. There's a reassuring permanence, a welcome, drama-free normality to turning up in the newsroom. On air I choose to wear a red dress, because I feel bold and on top of the world that the harshest treatment is over and some semblance of routine is returning. I can really crack on now.

Wednesday 25 May [2016]
On 31 July 2015 I was diagnosed with breast cancer. One mastectomy, six sessions of chemotherapy and thirty doses of radiotherapy later, I feel like this could be a fresh start. I know not everybody gets the opportunity, I'm completely aware of that, and so very grateful. Exceptionally grateful.
Huge sigh.
OK.
Pause. Smile.
It's time to crack on with the rest of my life.

Diary entries from *Dear Cancer*, 2017 | Victoria Derbyshire (b.1968)

I am only one,
But still I am one.
I cannot do everything,
But I can still do something;
And because I cannot do everything,
I will not refuse to do the something that I can do.

Helen Keller (1880–1968)

'You have to eat life or life will eat you.'

Joan Collins (b.1933)

If I were going to make my life a happy one, I'd have to do it on my own. That may be why at age 11, I made the calculated decision to quit acting pissed off at my glasses and hearing aids and use them instead as comic props. ... By the time I was 12, I had cemented my reputation as a class clown with a temper and a streak of the wild. It would take me another two years before I'd slow down on the tricks enough to reawaken to my own body and realize I could use all that excess of feeling as a different way to hear.

From *Mean Little Deaf Queer: A Memoir*, 2009 | Terry Galloway (b.1950)

'I do not regret my situation, I thank God that he has been pleased to make me as I am, nor do I envy the enjoyment of others.'

Sarah Biffin, *disabled professional miniaturist who signed her work 'painted by Miss Biffin Without Hands'* (1781–1850)

That I not be a restless ghost
Who haunts your footsteps as they pass
Beyond the point where you have left
Me standing in the newsprung grass,

You must be free to take a path
Whose end I feel no need to know,
No irking fever to be sure
You went where I would have you go...

So you can go without regret
Away from this familiar land,
Leaving your kiss upon my hair
And all the future in your hands.

From *Blackberry Winter: My Earlier Years*, 1972 | Margaret Mead (1901–1978) to her daughter

Who knows what women can be when they are finally free to become themselves?

From *The Feminine Mystique*, 1963 | Betty Friedan (1921–2006)

...in those moments, when we don't think we're smart enough, or pretty enough, or skinny enough, or successful enough, or basically just not enough, I had a woman say to me: 'Just know you will never be enough, but you can know the value of your worth if you just put down the measuring stick.'

From Golden Globe acceptance speech, 6 January 2025 | Demi Moore (b.1962)

...in those moments, when we don't think we're smart enough, or pretty enough, or skinny enough, or successful enough, or basically just not enough, I had a woman say to me: 'Just know you will never be enough, but you can know the value of your worth if you just put down the measuring stick.'

From Golden Globe acceptance speech, 6 January 2025 | Demi Moore (b.1962)

'After all, tomorrow is another day.'

From *Gone With the Wind*, 1936 | Margaret Mitchell (1900–1949)

I take a breath, and realize I've only asked [my mother] two questions and she already looks pretty tired! But I'm on a roll now – there's no way she's going to bed until we've smashed the fuck out of this glass ceiling!

ME: So, Mum, what do you want for women in the future?

MUM/YVONNE: I want my three granddaughters to be on a level playing field from day one. I want it to be illegal to discriminate. And don't just say wages are going to be equal – do it now. I want them to be treated with respect, and be equal without asking for it. I want things to move forward.

I press STOP.

One day my daughters might be interviewing me. Will it be the same conversation?

I fucking hope not.

From 'An Interview with My Mum' in *Feminists Don't Wear Pink (and other lies)*, curated by Scarlett Curtis, 2018 | Jodie Whittaker, *first woman Doctor Who* (b.1982)

My life has been long, and believing that life loves the liver of it, I have dared to try many things, sometimes trembling, but daring, still. I have only included here events and lessons which I have found useful. I have not told how I have used the solutions, knowing that you are intelligent and creative and resourceful and you will use them as you see fit...

You may not control all the events that happen to you, but you can decide not to be reduced by them. Try to be a rainbow in someone's cloud. Do not complain. Make every effort to change things you do not like. If you cannot make a change, change the way you have been thinking. You might find a new solution.

Never whine. Whining lets a brute know that a victim is in the neighbourhood.

Be certain that you do not die without having done something wonderful for humanity.

I gave birth to one child, a son, but I have thousands of daughters. You are Black and White, Jewish and Muslim, Asian, Spanish-speaking, Native American and Aleut. You are fat and thin and pretty and plain, gay and straight, educated and unlettered, and I am speaking to you all. Here is my offering to you.

From the foreword, *Letter to My Daughter*, 2008 |
Maya Angelou (1928–2014)

SOURCES

Margery Allingham, *The Fashion in Shrouds* (1938), Heinemann.

Margery Allingham, *The Beckoning Lady* (1955), Chatto & Windus.

Stacy Allison, *Beyond the Limits* (1994), Little, Brown.

Maya Angelou, *Letter to My Daughter* (2009), Penguin Random House.

Maya Angelou, 'Weekend Glory' in *Phenomenal Women* (1979), Penguin Random House.

Maya Angelou, 'Phenomenal Women' in *Phenomenal Women* (1979), Penguin Random House.

Maya Angelou, 'And Still I Rise' in *Phenomenal Women* (1979), Penguin Random House.

Lady Cynthia Asquith, *Remember And Be Glad* (1952), James Barrie.

Margaret Atwood, *The Handmaid's Tale* (1998) Vintage.

Excerpt from CAT'S EYE by Margaret Atwood, copyright © 1988 by O. W. Toad, Ltd. Used by permission of Doubleday, an imprint of the Knopf Doubleday Publishing Group, a division of Penguin Random House LLC. All rights reserved.

Excerpt(s) from CAT'S EYE by Margaret Atwood, Copyright © 1988 O.W. Toad Ltd. Reprinted by permission of Emblem/McClelland & Stewart, a division of Penguin Random House Canada Limited. All rights reserved; Hachette UK.

Jane Austen, *Jane Austen's Letters* (2011), Oxford Publishing Limited, reproduced with permission of the Licensor through PLSclear.

Joan Baez, *Daybreak: An Intimate Journal* (1971), Harper Collins.

Enid Bagnold, *National Velvet* (2017), Farshore.

Elif Batuman, *The Idiot* (2019), Penguin Books; Vintage.

Lesley Blanch, *The Wilder Shore of Love* (2010), W&N.

Elizabeth Bowen, English Novelists (1945), Collins.

Elizabeth Bowen, *Collected Impressions* (1950), Longmans Green & Co, reproduced with permission of Curtis Brown Group Ltd, London, on behalf of the Literary Executors of the Estate of Elizabeth Bowen.

Simone de Beauvoir, *A Very Easy Death* translated by Patrick O'Brian Deitsch (1969), Penguin Random House.

Simone de Beauvoir, *The Second Sex* (1972), Penguin Modern Classics.

Vera Brittain and Winifred Holtby, *Between Friends* (2022), Virago.

© Rosellen Brown, *Cora Fry* (1977), W W Norton & Co.

Pearl S Buck, *To My Daughter*, With Love (1967), John Day Co.

Candace Bushnell, *Sex and the City* (1996), Grove Atlantic; Hachette.

Karen Cheung, *The Impossible City: A Hong Kong Memoir* (2022), Random House Inc.

Agatha Christie, *Three Act Tragedy* (2016), Harper Collins.

Agatha Christie, *The Hollow* (2015), Harper Collins.

Agatha Christie, *The Man in the Brown Suit* (2017), Harper Collins.

Agatha Christie, *An Autobiography* (2017), Harper Collins.

Lady Anne Clifford, *Diaries* (2009), The History Press.

Lucille Clifton, *Two-Headed Woman* (1980), University of Massachusetts.

Lucille Clifton, "won't you celebrate with me" from *The Book of Light*. Copyright © 1993 by Lucille Clifton. Reprinted with the permission of The Permissions Company, LLC on behalf of Copper Canyon Press, coppercanyonpress.org.

Shirley Conran, *Superwoman in Action* (1979), Penguin Random House.

Shirley Conran, *Superwoman 2* (1977), Sidgwick & Jackson.

Amanda Craig, *The Three Graces* (2023), Abacus. Reproduced with permission of the Licensor through PLSclear.

Eve Curie, *Madame Curie* (1937), Doubleday.

© Rachel Cusk, *A Life's Work* (2019), Faber and Faber Ltd; Picador.

Extract from *Is There A Nutmeg in the House* by Elizabeth David by kind permission of the publisher, Grub Street.

Bette Davis, *This 'N' That* (1987), Sigdwick & Jackson.

Victoria Derbyshire, *Dear Cancer: A diary of hope to help your through* (2018), Trapeze.

Isla Dewar, *Women Talking Dirty* (1996), Headline.

Excerpt from LET ME TELL YOU WHAT I MEAN by Joan Didion, compilation copyright

© 2021 by Joan Didion. Used by permission of Alfred A. Knopf, an imprint of the Knopf

Doubleday Publishing Group, a division of Penguin Random House LLC. All rights reserved.; 4th Estate.

SOURCES

Jenny Diski, *Skating to Antarctica* (2005), Virago.

Daphne du Maurier, *Rebecca* (2015), Virago. Reproduced with permission of Curtis Brown Ltd, London, on behalf of The Chichester Partnership. Copyright © 1938 The Chichester Partnership.

Enheduana translated by Sophus Hell (2023), Yale University Press.

'Griselda' from *The Little Bookroom* by Eleanor Farjeon © Eleanor Farjeon, 1955, published by Henry Z. Walck, reproduced by kind permission by David Higham Associates.

Elena Ferrante Incidental Inventions – Europa Editions, 2019

Excerpt from BRIDGET JONES'S DIARY by Helen Fielding, copyright © 1996 by Helen Fielding. Used by permission of Viking Books, an imprint of Penguin Publishing Group, a division of Penguin Random House LLC. All rights reserved.

MFK Fisher, *The Gastronomical Me* (1989), North Point Press.

Marilyn French, *The Women's Room* (1997), Virago.

Nancy Friday, *My Mother, My Self* (1997), Random House Publishing Group.

Betty Freidan, *The Feminine Mystique* (2010), Penguin Classics.

Used with permission of Beacon Pr, from *Mean Little Deaf Queer* by Terry Galloway (2009); permission conveyed through Copyright Clearance Center, Inc.

Ava Gardner, *Ava: My Story* (1990), Bantam.

Lady Beatrice Glenavy, *Today We Will Only Gossip* (1964), Constable & Co.

Stella Gibbons, *Cold Comfort Farm* (2020), Penguin Classics.

© Elizabeth Gilbert, 2006, *Eat, Pray, Love*, Bloomsbury Publishing Plc.; Penguin Random House.

Selected quotes by Elizabeth Gilbert in *Body + Soul* magazine, 16 January 2025, copyright © 2025, Elizabeth Gilbert, used by permission of The Wylie Agency (UK) Limited.

Elizabeth Gilbert, 'Why I Cut My Hair Off' in Oprah Daily, 18 September 2024.

© Elizabeth Gilbert, 2010, *Committed*, Bloomsbury Publishing Plc.; Penguin Random House.

Selected quotes by Elizabeth Gilbert. Copyright © 2025, Elizabeth Gilbert, used by permission of The Wylie Agency (UK) Limited.

Elizabeth Goudge, *The Little White Horse* (2020), Lion Fiction. Reprinted with the permission of David Highams Associates Ltd on behalf of the copyright holder.

Linda Grant, *The Thoughtful Dresser* (2009), Virago. Reproduced with permission of the Licensor through PLSclear.

© Germaine Greer, *The Female Eunuch* (1970), MacGibbon & Kee; Harper Perrenial Modern Classics.

© Sheila Hancock, 2022, *Old Rage*, Bloomsbury Publishing Plc.

Excerpts from THE TRUTHS WE HOLD: AN AMERICAN JOURNEY by Kamala Harris, copyright © 2019 by Kamala D. Harris. Used by permission of Penguin Press, an imprint of Penguin Publishing Group, a division of Penguin Random House LLC. All rights reserved.

Kamala Harris, *The Truths We Hold: An American Journey* (2019), Penguin Random House; Penguin Publishing Group.

Diana Henry, *How to Eat a Peach* (2018), Mitchell Beazley.

Mrs Robert Henrey, *The Dream Makers* (1961), J.M. Dent & Sons.

Bell Hooks, *All About Love* (2018), William Morrow Paperbacks.

Dorothea Hosie, *The Pool of Ch'ien Lung* (1948), Hodder & Stoughton.

Zora Neale Hurston, *Dust Tracks on a Road: An Autobiography* (2020), Virago; Amistad.

© Erica Jong, 1997, *How to Save Your Own Life*, Bloomsbury Publishing Plc.; Tarcher.

Susan Kenney, *Between Friends: Writing Women Celebrate Friendship*, edited by Mickey Pearlman (1994), Houghton Mifflin. Licensed by permission of Susan Kenney, author, Charles A. Dana Professor of Creative Writing Emeritus, Colby College.

Excerpt from THE WOMAN WARRIOR: MEMOIRS OF A GIRLHOOD AMONG GHOSTS by Maxine Hong Kingston, copyright © 1975, 1976 by Maxine Hong Kingston. Used by permission of Alfred A. Knopf, an imprint of the Knopf Doubleday Publishing Group, a division of Penguin Random House LLC. All rights reserved.

Judith Krantz, *Princess Daisy* (1980), Sidgwick & Jackson.

© Nella Last, *Nella Last's War* (1983), Profile Books.

© Nella Last, *Nella Last's Peace* (2008), Profile Books.

© Nella Last, *Nella Last in the 1950s* (2010), Profile Books.

Nigella Lawson, *How to Eat* (1998), Chatto & Windus.

Excerpt(s) from THE LEFT HAND OF DARKNESS: 50TH ANNIVERSARY EDITION by Ursula K. Le Guin, copyright © 1969 by Ursula K. Le Guin. Used by permission of Ace, an imprint of Penguin Publishing Group, a division of Penguin Random House LLC. All rights reserved; Gollancz.

Rosamond Lehmann, *Invitation to the Waltz* (2006), Virago.

Deborah Levy, *The Cost of Living* (2018), Hamish Hamilton.

Anne Morrow Lindbergh, *Hour of Gold Hour of Lead* (1973), Elsevier Books Limited. Reproduced with permission of the Licensor through PLSclear.

Anne Lister, *I Know My Own Heart* (1988), Virago. Reproduced with permission of the Licensor through PLSclear.

Audre Lorde, 'Black Mother Woman', from *A Land Where Other People Live* (1973), Broadside Press.

From *The Collected Poems of Audre Lorde* © 1997 by Audre Lorde.

Evanna Lynch, 'Cat Woman' in *Feminists Don't Wear Pink* (2018), Penguin.

Shirley MacLaine, *My Lucky Stars: A Hollywood Memoir* (2011), Bantam.

Nadezhda Mandelstam, *Hope Abandoned* translated by Max Hayward (1974), Harvill Secker.

Katherine Mansfield, *Katherine Mansfield's Letters to John Middleton Murray* (1951), Constable.

Katherine Manfield, *Katherine Mansfield and Virginia Woolf* (2018), Edinburgh University Press. Reproduced with permission of the Licensor through PLSclear.

Hilary Mantel, *Beyond Black* (2023), 4th Estate; Picador.

Extract from *West with the Night* by Beryl Markham reprinted by permission of Pollinger Limited (www.pollingerlimited.com) on behalf of the estate of Beryl Markham.

From *Amortality* by Catherine Mayer published by Vermilion. Copyright © Catherine Mayer 2011. Reprinted by permission of The Random House Group Limited.

Margaret Mead, *Blackberry Winter* (1971), William Morrow.

Clara Milburn, *Mrs Milburn's diaries 1939–1945* (1981), Harper Collins.

Nancy Mitford, *The Pursuit of Love* (1945), Hamish Hamilton.

Nancy Mitford, *Love from Nancy: The Love Letters of Nancy Mitford* (1994), Sceptre.

Toni Morrison, *Sula* (1973), Virago; Vintage.

Catherine Newman, *We All Want Impossible Things* (2022), Doubleday.

Anaïs Nin, *Henry and June* (2001), Penguin.

Joyce Carol Oates, *The Journal of Joyce Carol Oates 1973–1982* (2007), Ecco.

Michelle Obama, *Becoming* (2021), Crown; Penguin.

From LOVINGLY, GEORGIA: Complete Correspondence of Georgia O'Keefe & Anita Pollitzer by edited by Clive Giboire. Copyright © 1991 by The Estate of Georgia O'Keefe. Copyright 1991 by the Estate of Anita Pollitzer. Reprinted with the permission of Touchstone, an imprint of Simon & Schuster LLC. All rights reserved.

With kind permission from Susie Orbach and Luise Eichenbaum for the extract from *Bittersweet: Love, Competition & Envy in Women's Friendships*, Century, London 1987, released as Between Women, Penguin Viking, New York 1988.

Dorothy Parker, *Enough Rope* (2022), Ragged Hand.

Christina Patterson, *The Art of Not Falling Apart* (2018), Atlantic.

Extract from *I Don't Know How She Does It* by Allison Pearson reprinted by permission of Peters Fraser & Dunlop (www.petersfraserdunlop.com) on behalf of Allison Pearson.; Knopf.

© Sylvia Plath, *Johnny Panic and the Bible of Dreams: and other prose writings* (1979), Faber and Faber Ltd.

© Sylvia Plath, *The Bell Jar* (2005), Faber and Faber Ltd.

Ruth Picardie, *Before I Say Goodbye* (1998), Penguin Random House.

Beatrix Potter, *The Journal of Beatrix Potter 1881–1897* (1989), Penguin Random House.

© Nina Mingya Powles, *Tiny Moons: A Year of Eating in Shanghai* (2020), The Emma Press Pamphlets.

Barbara Pym, *The Sweet Dove Died* (1978), Macmillan. Barbara Pym Estate, copyright ORL Co Ltd.

Barbara Pym, *Less Than Angels* (1955), Jonathon Cape. Barbara Pym Estate, copyright ORL Co Ltd.

Barbara Pym, Some Tame Gazelle (2022), Virago. Barbara Pym Estate, copyright ORL Co Ltd.

Jean Rhys, *Good Morning Midnight* (2000), Penguin Classics.

From OF WOMAN BORN: Motherhood as Experience and Institution by Adrienne Rich. Copyright © 1986, 1976 by W. W. Norton & Company, Inc. Used by permission of W. W. Norton & Company, Inc.

© Ella Risbridger, 2019, *Midnight Chicken (& Other Recipes Worth Living For)*, Bloomsbury Publishing Plc.

Lady Sackville, *Lady Sackville – A Biography by Susan Mary Alsop* (1978), Hachette.

Vita Sackville-West, *The Letters of Vita Sackville West and Virginia Woolf* (1992), Penguin Random House. Reproduced with permission of Curtis Brown Group Ltd, London on behalf of The Beneficiaries of the Estate of Vita Sackville West. Copyright © Vita Sackville West.

Vita Sackville-West, *Vita and Harold* (1992), Weidenfeld. Reproduced with permission of Curtis Brown Group Ltd, London on behalf of The Beneficiaries of the Estate of Vita Sackville West. Copyright © Vita Sackville West.

Vita Sackville-West, *The Life of Vita Sackville-West by Philippe Julia* (1976), Hamish Hamilton. Reproduced with permission of Curtis Brown Group Ltd, London on behalf of The Beneficiaries of the Estate of Vita Sackville West. Copyright © Vita Sackville West.

Vita Sackville-West, *A Week in France with Virginia* (1995), Palgrave Macmillan. Reproduced with permission of Curtis Brown Group Ltd, London on behalf of The Beneficiaries of the Estate of Vita Sackville West. Copyright © Vita Sackville West.

Vita Sackville-West, *The Land* (2004), Francis Lincoln. Reproduced with permission of Curtis Brown Group Ltd, London on behalf of The Beneficiaries of the Estate

of Vita Sackville West. Copyright © Vita Sackville West.

From RECOVERING, A JOURNAL by May Sarton. Copyright © 1980 by May Sarton. Used by permission of W. W. Norton & Company, Inc.; Open Road Media.

From JOURNAL OF A SOLITUDE by May Sarton. Copyright © 1973 by May Sarton. Used by permission of W. W. Norton & Company, Inc.; Open Road Media.

Dorothy L Sayers, *Gaudy Night* (2016), Hodder Paperbacks.

Excerpt from THE STONE DIARIES by Carol Shields, Copyright © 1993 Carol Shields. Reprinted by permission of Random House Canada, a division of Penguin Random House Canada Limited. All rights reserved.

Sei Shonagon, *The Pillow Book of Sei Shonagon* translated by Ivan Morris (1967), Columbia University Press.

© Jane Smiley, *A Year at the Races: Reflections on Horses, Humans, Love, Money & Luck* (2005), Faber and Faber Ltd.

Dodie Smith, *I Capture the Castle* (2004), Vintage.

Joan Smith, *Hungry for You* (1997), Vintage.

By Stevie Smith, from COLLECTED POEMS OF STEVIE SMITH, copyright ©1966 by Stevie Smith. Reprinted by permission of New Directions Publishing Corp; Faber and Faber Ltd.

Stevie Smith, *Novel On Yellow Paper* (1980), Virago. Reproduced with permission of the Licensor through PLSclear.

Stevie Smith, 'Autumn' in *Selected Poems* (2002), Penguin Modern Classics.

Susan Sontag, *As Consciousness is Harnessed to Flesh* (2012), Farrar, Straus & Giroux.

Muriel Spark, *The Prime of Miss Jean Brodie* (1961), Macmillan.

Gloria Steinem, *Outrageous Acts and Everyday Rebellions* (1984), Jonathan Cape.

Excerpt(s) from THE JOY LUCK CLUB by Amy Tan, copyright © 1989 by Amy Tan. Used by permission of G. P. Putnam's Sons, an imprint of Penguin Publishing Group, a division of Penguin Random House LLC. All rights reserved; Vintage.

Reprinted by permission of HarperCollins Publishers Ltd © *Where the Past Begins* (2017), Amy Tan.

THE OPPOSITE OF FATE by Amy Tan, copyright © 2003 by Amy Tan. Used by permission of G. P. Putnam's Sons, an imprint of Penguin Publishing Group, a division of Penguin Random House LLC. All rights reserved.; Reprinted by permission of HarperCollins Publishers Ltd © *The Opposite of Fate* (2004), Amy Tan.

Elizabeth Taylor, *At Mrs Lipincotes* (2011), Virago.

Alice B Toklas, *The Alice B. Toklas Cook Book* (1954), Harper & Brothers.

Alice Walker, *Gathering Blossoms Under Fire: The Journals of Alice Walker* edited by Valerie Boyd (2022), Weidenfeld & Nicolson.

Wendy Wasserstein, 'The Ties That Wound' in *Between Friends: Writing Women Celebrate Friendship* edited by Mickey Pearlman (1994), Houghton Mifflin.

Winifred Watson, *Miss Pettigrew Lives For a Day* (2008), Persephone Books. Used by permission of Persephone Books.

Rebecca Wells, *Divine Secrets of the Ya Ya Sisterhood* (1996), Harper Collins.

Jacqueline Wilson, *Best Friends* (2004), Doubleday Children.

Patricia Wentworth, *Pilgrim's Rest* (1948), Hachette.

Dorothy Whipple, *High Wages* (2009), Persephone Books. Used by permission of Persephone Books.

Oprah Winfrey, *Oprah Winfrey Speaks* (1998), John Wiley & Sons.

Copyright © 1981 by Merle Woo. From THIS BRIDGE CALLED MY BACK: WRITINGS BY RADICAL WOMEN OF COLOR, Fortieth Anniversary Edition, published by SUNY Press in 2021. All rights reserved. By permission of Stuart Bernstein Representation for Artists, New York, NY and protected by the Copyright Laws of the United States. All rights reserved. The printing, copying, redistribution, or retransmission of this Content without express permission is prohibited.

Virginia Woolf, *Selected Letters* (2008), Vintage.

Virginia Woolf, *Selected Diaries* edited by Anne Olivier Bell (2008), Vintage.

Virginia Woolf, *A Room of One's Own* (2020), Penguin Modern Classics.

Virginia Woolf, *To the Lighthouse* (2017), Macmillan Collector's Library.

Virginia Woolf, *Mrs Dalloway* (2020), Penguin Modern Classics.

Joan Wyndham, *Love is Blue: A Wartime Diary* (1987), Flamingo.

© Banana Yoshimoto, *Kitchen* (2018), Faber and Faber Ltd.

Excerpt from KITCHEN, copyright © 1988 by Banana Yoshimoto. Translation copyright © 1993 by Megan Backus. Used by permission of Grove/Atlantic, Inc. Any third- party use of this material, outside of this publication, is prohibited.

INDEX

A

B

C

D

E

F

G

H

J

K

L

ABOUT THE EDITOR

Sarah Gristwood is a biographer, journalist and commentator on royal affairs. Her previous books include the bestselling *Arbella: England's Lost Queen, The Tudors in Love: The Courtly Code Behind the Last Medieval Dynasty, Secret Voices: A Year of Women's Diaries* and biographies of Beatrix Potter, Winston Churchill, Vita Sackville-West and Virginia Woolf, and HM Queen Elizabeth II. She is a Fellow of the Royal Historical Society and the Royal Society of Arts. She regularly contributes to TV documentary series and news channels including CNN, Sky News and the BBC.

prevent breast cancer

Breast cancer is a devastating disease that affects too many people – patients, their families, friends and colleagues. It is a disease that can often be cured if caught early and suitable treatments are prescribed. But what if there was no need for the cure? If there was no diagnosis, no before or after breast cancer. What if people could live their lives safe in the knowledge that it would never happen to them?

Prevent Breast Cancer is the only UK charity entirely dedicated to the prediction and prevention of breast cancer.

Breast cancer remains the most common cancer in the UK, with over 56,800 people diagnosed each year. Breaking the cycle of breast cancer means thinking bigger, and that's why we're all-in on science to save lives. By promoting early diagnosis, screening, and lifestyle changes, we believe we can stop the problem before it starts.

Words therefore cannot fully express our gratitude for Sarah's generous donation from the publication of *Celebrating Women*. Her generosity continues to inspire and propel our efforts forward, exemplifying the power of female compassion and community.

For further information on how we're getting ahead of breast cancer, visit www.preventbreastcancer.org.uk.

(Reg. Charity number: 1109839)

First published in the United Kingdom
in 2025 by
Batsford
43 Great Ormond Street
London
WC1N 3HZ

An imprint of B. T. Batsford Holdings Limited

ISBN 9781837330041

A CIP catalogue record for this book is available from the British Library.

10 9 8 7 6 5 4 3 2 1

Reproduction by Rival Colour Ltd, UK
Printed by Toppan Leefung Printing International Ltd, China

This book can be ordered direct from the publisher at www.batsfordbooks.com, or try your local bookshop

Distributed throughout the UK and Europe by Abrams & Chronicle Books, 1 West Smithfield, London EC1A 9JU and 57 rue Gaston Tessier, 75166 Paris, France

www.abramsandchronicle.co.uk
info@abramsandchronicle.co.uk

MIX
Paper | Supporting responsible forestry
FSC® C104723
www.fsc.org